ASSENTING TO THE ETERNAL:

KINGDOM EXCHANGES REVEALED

CAROLYN CÔTÉ

Energion Publications
Gonzalez, FL
2015

ISBN10: 1-63199-217-1
ISBN13: 978-1-63199-217-9
Library of Congress Control Number: 2015951654

Energion Publications
P. O. Box 841
Gonzalez, FL 32560

energion.com
pubs@energion.com
850-525-3916

DEDICATION

I dedicate this book to the memory of my brother-in-law, Brent. Brent's life was changed forever the summer of 2013 when he suffered an accident, while swimming in the ocean, which left him paralyzed from the chin down. A word from the Lord given to his wife, Patty, in the elevator at Shock Trauma gave hope: *"Everything we lose is exchangeable for that which can never be lost."* In that elevator, in that moment, this book was born.

Brent was released from his earthly losses on February 25, 2015. He's missed. He was one of those easy to love individuals. He was funny, generous, kind and even after his accident, his vibrant, blue eyes still sparkled. For those of us yet subject to loss I know Brent would remind us of Paul's words to the Romans, *"For I consider that the sufferings of this present time are not worthy to be compared with the glory that is to be revealed to us."*

TABLE OF CONTENTS

Foreword

Surrender.

It's a word we often throw around in church these days but do we really understand what it means? The dictionary says it means to "stop fighting," "to let go," "to give up control." Those are great descriptors of what surrender in the Christian life is!

We give up OUR will, OUR rights, OUR demands, OUR plans, OUR pursuits … OUR kingdom. We surrender, not so that we can be empty and void, we surrender so that we may fully embrace the greatest kingdom that exists in the world: God's Kingdom. It's not a kingdom you will find in the center of religion. It's a kingdom you will discover in the middle of a revolution! A kingdom where men and women willingly throw down the broken pieces of their lives—their small kingdoms—at the foot of the cross to gain access to the King's Kingdom which truly transforms! In the pages to come, discover areas where your kingdom still stands and be willing to surrender … surrender to gain the greatness of the Kingdom of God.

Jim Larrabee
Lead Pastor
First Christian Church
Santa Maria, California

INTRODUCTION

The pain came on a regular weekday. It didn't come in doable waves like childbirth or kidney stone pain. This pain felt like an open wound in my stomach–raw and pounding, constant and debilitating. I hyperventilated trying to breathe it away. Seven doctors, multiple tests, and two years later, the pain remained a mystery. My four children grew. I withered to 93 pounds.

Sometimes the hard trials don't go away. You pray. You claim. You quote. You get others to pray, to claim, to quote. And when all your best Biblical Christian tools appear to fail, you cry for understanding, "God, what are You doing?"

> *"The silver is mine and the gold is mine, declares the LORD of hosts. The latter glory of this house will be greater than the former,"* says the LORD *of hosts, "and in this place I will give peace,"* declares the LORD *of hosts.*
>
> — Haggai 2:8-9

God's Kingdom work is within you. In you, He is building a living temple for His glory. Throughout the process, you are often fear-filled but somehow you know that absolute child-like dependence is your touchstone even when you don't understand God's plan. You can't run; nor can you stand passive.

You must lean-in.

Even though.

Even though you see only losses and grief.

Even though you feel like you may drown, alone, in your pain.

Even though the enemy of your soul asks you to question

God's magnificence.

Even though you despair of your youthfulness in the ways of the Kingdom of God.

Faith becomes your anchor to hope. Faith reminds you that there must be something of value in the testing, trial or tribulation. Faith gives you the fortitude to plod on through the darkest days, hopeful of eyes to see.

Take a look around you, right now, wherever you are. Pick something up and examine the underside. Sit under a table and look up. What do you see? Clues to the topside, yes, but nothing as magnificent. Nothing certainly to love and adore.

On this earth, you live on the underside, the preview, of the Godhead's power and magnificence. Your journey to the mature stature where the mind of Christ opens your eyes to perceive the topside, your situation in spirit and in truth, is what this book is about. Your journey—your narrow path—is the holy, plodding climb to where the height you acquire allows you to rise above and overcome everything you judge as bad. This is where you will experience the joy-filled state of the overcomer! Beloved Christian, you have been adopted into God's glorious Kingdom!

Your sonship, purchased by Christ, sets you apart to inherit imperishable riches and your inheritance begins:

Now.

But you're perplexed and frustrated by your life in God's Kingdom. I understand. Kingdom life is spiritual and unseen and its system of exchanges (commerce) is not only unexpected, it's unreasonable in its graciousness. Worst of all, your human nature does not prefer what God gives until experience gives you a sampling of the glory God longs to give you.

While you live on this earth, glory is imparted when you assent to exchanges. In the beginning, God's offerings won't be understood and you may resist because you lack the experience to recognize their worth. Fear not; though Christ longs to give you what He purchased, your inheritance, He is polite. He knocks and waits for your assent to bestow.

God is building something out of ashes, you see. He is building in you the fullness required for you to be a temple for His glory, the Bride of Christ!

Our light affliction, which is but for a moment, 'worketh for us a far more exceeding and eternal weight of glory.' The present is influencing the future. It is not for us to reason and philosophize about this, but to take God at His Word and believe it. Experience, feelings, observation of others, may seem to deny this fact. Ofttimes afflictions appear only to sour us and make us more rebellious and discontented. But let it be remembered that afflictions are not sent by God for the purpose of purifying the flesh: they are designed for the benefit of the "new man." Moreover, afflictions help to prepare us for the glory hereafter. Affliction draws away our heart from the love of the world; it makes us long more for the time when we shall be translated from this scene of sin and sorrow; it will enable us to appreciate (by way of contrast) the things which God has prepared for them that love Him. Here then is what faith is invited to do: to place in one scale the present affliction, in the other, the eternal glory. Are they worthy to be compared? No, indeed.

— A. W. Pink, *Comfort for Christians* (1886-1952)

"Peace I leave with you; My peace I give to you; not as the world gives do I give to you. Do not let your heart be troubled, nor let it be fearful."

— John 14:27

PART I
LAYING THE FOUNDATION WITH CHRIST ALONE

The Kingdom of God within you is built upon a foundation of firm and long lasting materials which are vital to the ability of your structure to overcome every season. If the foundations are not present or are severely faulty, the structure suffers–you suffer and therefore the Body of Christ suffers.

YOU: ASSENTING TO A NEW KINGDOM

To enter the Kingdom of God, your first Kingdom Exchange took place when you traded living in your sin nature for living in Christ. Though this process took place within you there were certain characteristics I'll illustrate using a short allegory:

Drawn by God, you longed for an exchange of the old for the new. You crossed the river separating you from your former life and stood on the opposite bank appraising the steep ascent to the impenetrable walls of God's Kingdom. John the Baptist stepped near and pointing upward to the entrance gate, he cried, "Behold the Lamb of God Who takes away the sin of the world."

Dripping wet, you were happy to make another exchange: faith in an unseen kingdom for life in that Kingdom. You ascended the path but when you reached the gate, the Lamb of God lay slain and bleeding at the entrance. His blood flowed toward you–a cleansing rivulet washing your dusty feet to allow your entrance by redeeming a nature unfit for God's Kingdom. You became a new creature. Your new eyes saw the resurrected Lamb of God and your new ears heard your name being read from His Book of Life. Running to Him, you bowed at His feet and for the first time since you were born, you experienced peace.

As a newborn babe, you began Kingdom life aware of God's mercy but naive of His mysteries. You knew God intended to build His Kingdom within you but in those early days you didn't concern yourself with how that would be accomplished. Ensconced in a comfortable nursery, you fed on the life-giving honey-sweet milk of the Word of Truth. You grew. And grew. Your teeth emerged and the day came when you outgrew the nursery. You were ready for weightier truths—for the meat that gives you the strength to become, "a mature man, to the measure of the stature which belongs to the fullness of Christ"(Ephesians 4:13).

What is that meat which strengthens you?

Tribulation.

> *Therefore, since Christ has suffered in the flesh, arm yourselves also with the same purpose, because he who has suffered in the flesh has ceased from sin, so as to live the rest of the time in the flesh no longer for the lusts of men, but for the will of God.*

> — 1 Peter 4:1-2

Tribulation comes for all Kingdom children; it separates you from your happy state, your normal state, your contented life. You pray, you expect to be released from tribulation's grasp but your prayers aren't answered. Though you know you should trust God regardless … most of the time … you don't.

May I suggest your spiritual symptoms?

A core disquiet nags at you.

Those you try to help don't truly get better.

Your life doesn't work and your work doesn't bring life.

Are you ready for a transforming truth?

Your seasons of testings, trials and tribulations are for your maturing! If you endure the process and assent to the exchanges they offer, authentic and eternal deposits and their resulting eternal works are your inheritance purchased by Christ.

YOU: ASSENTING TO ADOPTION BY GOD

From the foundations of the earth, God purposed that those who were not His chosen people would become the very sons of God. (1 Peter 2:10) God went so mercifully far as to blind the eyes of His chosen people (Romans 11) in order that when the fullness of time came, the Lamb who was slain from the foundations of the earth could purchase adoption for all of mankind (Galatians 3:6-14).

John the Baptist served as man's preparer to receive both faith and life. He embodied the old covenant–external righteousness. Then, Jesus takes external righteousness down:

> *"I say to you, among those born of women there is no one greater than John; yet he who is least in the kingdom of God is greater than he."*
>
> — Luke 7:28

You. You are greater than John the Baptist. You have advantages John didn't.

The Law, like John, came first to expose and oppose your inert, dusty self and to direct you down the straight path toward your nature's only possible end: a watery grave.

When you emerged, like a newborn babe, blinking your eyes against the light, John pointed to Christ and said, "This is He on behalf of whom I said, 'After me comes a Man who has a higher rank than I, for He existed before me'" (John 1:30).

"He must increase, but I must decrease" (John 3:30).

And John does decrease in order for you to enjoy internal righteousness–the very Spirit of God dwelling within.

When Christ who is the source of Life comes, the one-dimensional expression inscribed onto stone tablets by the finger of God is usurped, fulfilled by Life Himself. The stone wasn't intended to become bread for you; you need Living Bread. You need the wedding's inferior wine to be usurped by the excellent wine. You need the fruitless fig tree to be usurped by the plantings of the Lord that bear fruit regardless of the season. You need the Chief Cornerstone to usurp the temple made with hands with a new, everlasting expression of His glory made from living stones.

Honor the process: while you were yet carnal and submitted to the Law's tutelage there was none greater.

Now,

In Christ,

You are a child of the Kingdom of God.

And even the very least member of the Kingdom of God is greater than John. John suffers a renting decapitation and the veil separating God from His beloved is torn in two. The law, as head, is replaced by the One Who is the head which animates the Life of the body which is the church, His spiritual offspring.

*"But this is the covenant which I will make with the house
of Israel after those days," declares the LORD, "I will put My
law within them and on their heart I will write it; and I will
be their God, and they shall be My people. They will not teach
again, each man his neighbor and each man his brother, saying,
'Know the LORD,' for they will all know Me, from the least of
them to the greatest of them," declares the LORD, "for I will forgive their iniquity, and their sin I will remember no more."*

— Jeremiah 31:33-34

Your adoption secure, you are the deed holder to all that your
Heavenly Father gives His children. Not like this world gives, no.
God gives glory eternal and for you to cherish what He gives as
much as He loves to bestow it, you must endure the discipline
necessary to discern flesh and spirit.

*It is for discipline that you endure; God deals with you
as with sons; for what son is there whom his father does not
discipline? But if you are without discipline, of which all have
become partakers, then you are illegitimate children and not sons.
Furthermore, we had earthly fathers to discipline us, and we re-
spected them; shall we not much rather be subject to the Father of
spirits, and live? For they disciplined us for a short time as seemed
best to them, but He disciplines us for our good, so that we may
share His holiness. All discipline for the moment seems not to be
joyful, but sorrowful; yet to those who have been trained by it,
afterwards it yields the peaceful fruit of righteousness. Therefore,
strengthen the hands that are weak and the knees that are feeble,
and make straight paths for your feet, so that the limb which is
lame may not be put out of joint, but rather be healed.*

— Hebrews 12:7-13

Kingdom exchanges are vital! They are the means by which you obtain the full stature necessary to rule and reign with Christ.

Your seasons of testings, trials, and tribulations are your trading-up floor. If you endure and assent to the trade, eternal deposits and their resulting works are your inheritance through Christ.

YOU: ASSENTING TO A LIFE OF FAITH

It's time to get real before God. Like a storekeeper taking an inventory, you gaze at your barren shelves and confess, "I don't have anything left to rely upon, God. I don't appreciate this trial but I want to see it from Your perspective."

With that relinquishing prayer:

Your will–you give up.

Your dreams–you let die.

It feels both terrifying and courageous ... and proper.

Clutching your passport of faith, you become an explorer discovering your new, often confusing Kingdom. You don't know the language. You don't have a map. And yet, you press on through the difficult terrain willing to listen and learn from your guide, the Holy Spirit. He is all you need to navigate; He is your interpreter, your comforter and your teacher.

Rich or poor, you entered God's Kingdom with the spiritual understanding that you were bankrupt–completely dependent on Christ's sacrifice as the entrance payment. Your confusion began almost at once. What do I do here? How do I get what I need and want here? How do I succeed here? How do I get wealthy here?

This earthly realm does not serve as your tutor for the Kingdom of God. That is, unless you use it to find Matthew 5's antonyms. Here, wealth is a process of accumulation. In the Kingdom of God, filling your shelves is the opposite. It is those who acknowledge their spiritual poverty who inherit the Kingdom of God.

Commerce is also polar opposite in the Kingdom of God. In the earthly realm, a good trade is one which gains you an equal or better value. In the Kingdom of God, a good exchange is our 1 for God's 100. A very few examples:

Our deadly nature exchanged for a living nature.

Our simple confession of faith in Christ's sufficiency exchanged for an eternity of fellowship with God.

Our bondage exchanged for Christ's yoke and a rested soul.

Our becoming last exchanged to become first.

Although from God's perspective these exchanges must appear unfairly unequal, inside the values of the Godhead they're wholly satisfying. Your childlike dependency and your confession of inability are the only human currency needed to obtain treasure in the Kingdom of God.

For a king to have a kingdom, servants know their proper place. You knew this, you thought. But now you know something better–servants don't require their king to carry out their short-sighted will or their smallish dreams. When the King is God, His will is trusted and preferred because His values are the exquisite treasures of your new Kingdom and those treasures are in keeping with the highest form of love–love toward you as an individual and love toward His people as a corporate body.

YOU: STUDYING GOD'S BLUEPRINTS FOR HIS KINGDOM

What is God building?

ZION

Then I looked, and behold, the Lamb was standing on Mount Zion, and with Him one hundred and forty-four thousand, having His name and the name of His Father written on their foreheads. And I heard a voice from heaven, like the sound of many waters and like the sound of loud thunder, and the voice which I heard was like the sound of harpists playing on their harps. And they sang a new song before the throne and before the four living creatures and the elders; and no one could learn the song except the one hundred and forty-four thousand who had been purchased from the earth. These are the ones who have not been defiled with women, for they have kept themselves chaste. These are the ones who follow the Lamb wherever He goes. These

have been purchased from among men as first fruits to God and
to the Lamb. And no lie was found in their mouth; they are
blameless.

— Revelation 14:1-5

God is building a people, a city set on a hill, lit only with His glory. You, His child, are one stone among many that support one another to comprise His living temple. Your natural form is chiseled to fit what He is building so that by the end of this present age we will be prepared to rule and reign with Him after the final casting out of Satan and his demons from heaven (1 Corinthians 3:9).

In your obedience to the leadings of the Holy Spirit, your spiritual callings and gifts serve the purposes of God's Kingdom. The more you obey, the more you will be entrusted with higher responsibilities. But be aware–you don't use your calling and gifts to serve God's Kingdom, your calling uses you.

This state of usefulness is what Paul refers to as becoming a living sacrifice—consecrated to His purposes without thought to the interests of self.

> *"For this reason I say to you, do not be worried about your*
> *life, as to what you will eat or what you will drink; nor for your*
> *body, as to what you will put on. Is not life more than food, and*
> *the body more than clothing? Look at the birds of the air, that*
> *they do not sow nor reap nor gather into barns, and yet your*
> *heavenly Father feeds them. Are you not worth much more than*
> *they? And who of you by being worried can add a single hour to*
> *his life? And why are you worried about clothing? Observe how*
> *the lilies of the field grow; they do not toil nor do they spin, yet I*

*say to you than not even Solomon in all his glory clothed himself
like one of these. But if God so clothes the grass of the field, which
is alive today and tomorrow is thrown into the furnace, will He
not much more clothe you? You of little faith! Do not worry then,
saying, 'What will we eat?' or 'What will we drink?' or 'What
will we wear for clothing?' For the Gentiles eagerly seek all these
things; for your heavenly Father knows that you need all these
things. But seek first His kingdom and His righteousness, and all
these things will be added to you."*

— Matthew 6:25-33

Worry is only a symptom—a symptom of a divided heart. Your attempts to not worry are futile or temporary until you undergo a loss which brings revelation. Fear not! The Father is pleased to give you the Kingdom. As you grow to recognize its mysterious ways, worry will fall away as symptoms always do when their source is gone. You will grasp the vital Kingdom principle of the lilies of the field and the birds of the air. They conform to the set path the creator has created them to express:

If they are meant to be a single color or many colors

If they are meant to live a day or a week or a month or many years

If they are meant to emit a sweet perfume or a cheerful song

Both the lilies and the birds live out a worry-free, active existence which gives glory to the One who instilled in each a set, predetermined existence. How much more with you, the child He has gifted with a calling?

The promise is clear. You can assent to the process necessary to trust your King to provide or you can live as one with little faith.

With the two options set before you, as a child of the Kingdom of God, you barely hesitate. Like the widow entering the temple you deposit your mite into the temple treasury. As a spiritual widow of this world, you give of your very living to gain much more.

"Fear not little flock. The Father is pleased to give you the kingdom."

With God's order honored, your focus on the Kingdom of God frees you from the worries of directing your own life. You stop twisting and find the yoke is easy and light. Each day, you rise with your heart settled to live out God's will for the present day. Without thought for tomorrow, your daily work in this realm becomes a necessary, supporting structure to all that God's will is working in the earth. You eat, drink, work and rest with single-mindedness. Without conscious effort you are the light of the world; you are the salt of the earth.

Though you will never forget your season of loss, it will be forever settled in your heart that what you gained eternally outweighed your losses.

YOU: ASSENTING TO SPIRITUAL WORKS

This realm's work-for-success path tripped you up for a while. You thought that if you worked hard for God's Kingdom you would be blessed. Instead, you've got troubles. Like the prodigal's elder brother, you question what's going on. You didn't even get a goat-roast party! Let the Father put his arm around you and explain, "All I have is yours. I don't want you to work for me. You are not my hired hand. I want to give you much more. You are my son."

To unlearn work-for-hire, Wall Street's trading-floor might be a useful analogy. All those caffeinated folks checking their monitors and yelling million dollar trades into headsets; trades they hope will net their employers profits. Likewise, in a popular board game, pastel-colored money is traded for property and houses netting rent payments from all players landing on said property. In the end, both Wall Street and the game of Monopoly® are the same: the losers (and the winners) pack up the metaphors and net exactly: nothing.

As described in the Apostle Paul's letter to the church at Corinth, children of the Kingdom of God can be builders of perishable things and go on to suffer a similar net loss:

> *Now if any man builds on the foundation with gold, silver, precious stones, wood, hay, straw, each man's work will become evident; for the day will show it because it is to be revealed with fire, and the fire itself will test the quality of each man's work. If any man's work which he has built on it remains, he will receive a reward. If any man's work is burned up, he will suffer loss; but he himself will be saved, yet so as through fire.*

— 1 Corinthians 3:12-15

It's reassuring that your adoption into the Kingdom of God cannot be lost but it's unsettling that what you build on that foundation can be lost. You can enter heaven with exactly: nothing.

So how do you work for God? Do you consider what Jesus might do? Do you scour the Bible for a command you'd like to obey? Do you think of what God might like done and do it?

No ... no ... no.

In this realm–your old nature, works.

In God's Kingdom–your new nature, obeys.

In this realm, work begins in the mind, the hands and the feet expend energy, sweat is sweated and in exchange, something tangible comes into existence.

In the Kingdom of God, work is inspired by the Holy Spirit. Your heart listens, your mind assents and your strength chooses to obey. This is how you express your love of God. At times when you lack faith and judge God's command as onerous you may struggle to obey but once you agree to perform His will, these blessings are yours:

Grace to perform the work.

Christ is your yoke-mate.

Fruit. Fruit that remains.

When you choose not to obey, the Holy Spirit is long-suffering. He often gives you more than one chance. You will hear His soft reminders as does He hear your replies. If you still don't obey, you will unlearn your attachment to your own will through suffering.

Fruit, precious stones and precious metals are beautiful and instructive metaphors of spiritual work. Fruit represents those lasting works which are an outward sign of the Spirit's inner workings. When you assent to the exchange of your works for God's works through you, you become the fertile soil where the riches you've inherited through Christ mature and produce eternal fruit. Jesus explained,

> *"Abide in Me, and I in you. As the branch cannot bear fruit of itself unless it abides in the vine, so neither can you unless you*

abide in Me. I am the vine, you are the branches; he who abides
in Me and I in him, he bears much fruit, for apart from Me you
can do nothing."

— John 15:4-5

"For apart from Me you can do nothing."

As in fruit, so also in precious metals and stones. Once again, when you assent to the exchange, your afflictions become the hidden super-heated processes which produce rare treasure. Isaiah prophesied, "Behold, I have refined you, but not as silver; I have tested you in the furnace of affliction" (Isaiah 48:10). The Apostle Paul concurred when he prophesied over the church at Rome, "... and if children, heirs also, heirs of God and fellow heirs with Christ, if indeed we suffer with Him so that we may also be glorified with Him. For I consider that the sufferings of this present time are not worthy to be compared with the glory that is to be revealed to us" (Romans 8:17-18).

The process doesn't feel good; your world appears upside down, unrecognizable. Anxiety and depression leave you weak and shamed. The temporal shadow you'd settled for is unveiled allowing you to discover God's offering of more–true and lasting answers. The day you open your Bible to the book of Job, you not only find a fellow-sufferer, you find the faithfulness to agree with him:

"Naked I came from my mother's womb,
And naked I shall return there.
The LORD gave and the LORD has taken away.
Blessed be the name of the LORD."

— Job 1:21

For those of you who possess a natural fortitude, the process may take more time. Your strong will and high tolerance for pain allow you to grasp even tighter to your trusted formulas. You read hope-filled, how-to books looking for strategies to control God. This practice works for short periods of time and then, it doesn't.

In either case, in time, revelation comes and your love for God beckons you to consider His recorded ways. The Israelite's time in the wilderness captures your attention. It becomes a lantern guiding you through the dark wilderness of loss and brokenness. You recognize a pattern. Your questions find some refreshing answers. Your season of sorrow wanes. The grace to let go and free-fall into God's will for you, though still scary, becomes strangely possible. You enter a light-filled space: joy.

This is how Kingdom Exchanges operate. This is where you die to find true life. This is where God's Kingdom's rules of governance depose your tyrant-corpse in order that your spirit can mature into the foreordained, glory-filled Bride of Christ.

This is where you begin to understand and appreciate:

Jesus did more work with His hands and feet disabled than any man has ever done.

For children of the Kingdom, work isn't the goal–glory is the goal. Glory is quantified by the eternal taking place within you and those to which you minister. This glory is protected; the gates of hell cannot prevail against it. It is immune from the destructive forces of war, imprisonment, decay and poor design.

> *But we all, with unveiled face, beholding as in a mirror*
> *the glory of the Lord, are being transformed into the same image*
> *from glory to glory, just as from the Lord, the Spirit.*
>
> — 2 Corinthians 3:18

Under these circumstances, work takes on certain character-istics:

You follow and obey the Spirit's leading.

You trust the Mind of Christ more than your own thoughts.

You work the works of Christ and even greater works because He advocates on your behalf before the Father.

The results are to God's glory:

Fruit that remains

Gold

Silver

Precious stones

For the Father's will to be obeyed on earth as it is obeyed by the angels in heaven, it must be full of the faith which obeys fully and without question. This kind of obedience answers your oft prayed prayer: "Thy kingdom come thy will be done on earth as it is in heaven."

Not outward things, but inward. Not what a man eats and drinks, not where he lives, nor what is his nationality, nor the customs of his race, not even what he thinks nor what he says; but what are the inward characteristics of his nature, and the inward power of his spiritual life. For these alone consti-tute this kingdom of God. Not what I do, but what I am, is to decide whether I belong to it or not. And only as inward righteousness, and inward peace, and inward joy, and inward power are bestowed and experienced, can this kingdom be set up. Therefore no outward subjugation can accomplish results

like these, but only the interior work of the all-subduing spirit
of God.

— Hannah Whitall Smith (1832-1911)

The Christian's Secret of a Happy Life

YOU: ASSENTING TO PRUNING

You weren't empty handed when you stepped into His Kingdom; you brought with you your corpse, your flesh, your carnal
nature. Almost at once, the old and the new natures showed themselves in conflict. And yet, mixing both natures, especially when
serving God, proved easy. Though this is expected, in order for you
to mature in your ability to hear and obey the Holy Spirit the time
came for you to enter a new classroom: John 15. There, the con-
trasts between the flesh and spirit were exposed as two kingdoms
apart and unmixable.

When you assent to pruning, you lose something dead to gain
something alive. You sense something, something separate from
your flesh–something living, gaining ground: Life Himself. And
the more you choose Life the less death reigns in your mortal body.

Still, you hesitate, unsure. You worry, you wonder, Can I trust
Him?

A better question: Can I trust myself?

Much of what you suffer becomes an efficient shortcut to expose your divided heart. Self-reflection allows you to identify the
decisions which took you off the narrow path. The fog-like mist
enveloping your discernment lifts and the light you were miss-
ing shows you the way forward. The repenting of your own will

becomes a sweet smelling sacrifice, burning away the carnal and unnecessary, leaving the holy individual God purposed you to be.

You've often used your own strength to get through challenges. Your past accomplishments comforted you when you were afraid. You had affection for your good ideas. You trusted:

You.

Now, you must lose this misplaced self-trust.

> *At that time the disciples came to Jesus and said, "Who then is greatest in the kingdom of heaven?"*
>
> *And He called a child to Himself and set him before them, and said, "Truly I say to you, unless you are converted and become like children, you will not enter the kingdom of heaven. Whoever then humbles himself as this child, he is the greatest in the kingdom of heaven."*
>
> — Matthew 18:1-4

Your adult strength is the greatest barrier to you becoming great in the Kingdom of God.

Weakness, physical and emotional, is purposed to open your eyes to the humbling but healing truth: you weren't created to be independent. Your inability to make living choices was further hampered by that deadly something you inherited from your Eden parents: the ability to discern good and evil.

But now, because you have faith in Christ's sacrifice you are God's child–God's beloved child. His Son has become to you the other tree, the Tree of Life. His Kingdom, now within, is moving you toward the maturity where your heart, mind, soul and strength will proclaim that God is your all in all, the Alpha and Omega, the beginning and the end!

Maybe, for the first time, you see yourself clearly. You see how your lack of confidence in God has put you in an impossible position.

Will you exchange your natural self-confidence for child-like dependency? Even if the prospect is terrifying?

Yes, yes you will.

You run to God in surrender and make your offer:

Your strength exchanged for God's strength.

Rejoice! With the dead wood cut away, the Vine can now flow life to those cut ends and in due season they will bud forth with fruit that remains.

YOU: ASSENTING TO BECOMING AN OVERCOMER

Before we continue, it is vital for you to understand the on-going intercessions and accusations over and against you in the heavenlies.

Satan, forever jealous of the glorious nature you've been given, accuses you night and day before God. He blindly wagers with God that your devotion is blessings conditional. Christ, your High Priest, sits at your Father's right hand interceding on your behalf. Satan's desire to, "sift you as wheat" is countered with Christ's merciful prayer, "that your faith would fail not."

This contest places your two natures in the middle of a heavenly war purposed to display before all creation the supremacy of Christ's act of redemption. Christ's terms of buying back are clear: He promises to exchange everything Satan intends for death for a kingdom made up of those who love life more than death. (Romans 8:28)

Satan is playing the odds that Christ-followers are fair-weather worshippers. His end-of-the-age plan to gain the Bride of Christ's attention by powerful signs and wonders is intended to expose adulterous hearts more in love with gifts than they are with the Giver.

But not you. If your earthly life disintegrates, you won't be attracted to the signs and wonders of the anti-Christ. You won't forsake the lover of your soul for the hater of it.

No. You won't. Why? Because by the mercies of God you've suffered enough loss of the perishable to have lost your appetite for it; you count it all as loss. Only the knowledge of the sacrificial nature of Christ which lays down one's life for the sake of His Kingdom captures your heart. And though in your present trial you have prayed to have the bitter cup removed, you are willing to pray Christ's higher prayer, ". . . yet not as I will, but as You will."

As Christ acted in faith for the glory set before Him, so do you. You may not yet see but faith gives you a sureness, a confidence that a vista exists where you will perceive and enjoy God's Kingdom purposes. This being so, any tempting hesitation or resistance is unmasked as a saving of your life . . . only to lose it.

Rest assured of this one thing:

You will endure and you will overcome.

"Let us rejoice and be glad and give the glory to Him, for the marriage of the Lamb has come and His bride has made herself ready."

— Revelation 19:7

This hateful flesh of ours is a deep and subtle thing. It has to go if we are really to serve the purpose of God in fullness. Every bit of flesh has to meet the circumcising knife of the Cross. There can be no genuine work of the Spirit in any way save as the Cross meets us.

— John Wright Follette (1883-1966)

YOU: ASSENTING TO HUNGER AND THIRST

As a child of God's Kingdom, your own journey to expressing the fullness of God's love is full of seemingly incongruent experiences. You often feel confused and abandoned but you stay the course, faithful in spite of pain.

"Blessed are those who hunger and thirst for righteousness, for they shall be satisfied."

— Matthew 5:6

The Holy Spirit was given for your righteousness. Do you have empathy for His one desire to make you righteous?

You have not yet resisted to the point of shedding blood in your striving against sin; and you have forgotten the exhortation which is addressed to you as sons,

"My son, do not regard lightly the discipline of the Lord, nor faint when you are reproved by him; For those whom the Lord loves, he disciplines, And he scourges every son whom he receives."

It is for discipline that you endure; God deals with you as with sons; for what son is there whom his father does not discipline? But if you are without discipline, of which all have

become partakers, then you are illegitimate children and not sons.
Furthermore, we had earthly fathers to discipline us, and we re-
spected them; shall we not much rather be subject to the Father of
spirits, and live? For they disciplined us for a short time as seemed
best to them, but He disciplines us for our good, so that we may
share His holiness. All discipline for the moment seems not to be
joyful, but sorrowful; yet to those who have been trained by it,
afterwards it yields the peaceful fruit of righteousness.

— Hebrews 12:4-11

But you fail. You don't come up to the measure, the fullness
of a pure love. When you're reviled, you revile back. When you're
spoken evil of, you defend yourself. When your enemy takes your
coat, you take it back. You don't pray for the ones who have hurt
you. You long to be served much more than to serve. Righteousness
doesn't look like glory–it looks demeaning.

The Apostle Paul prays this for you,

For this reason I bow my knees before the Father, from
whom every family in heaven and on earth derives its name, that
He would grant you, according to the riches of His glory, to be
strengthened with power through His Spirit in the inner man, so
that Christ may dwell in your hearts through faith; and that you,
being rooted and grounded in love, may be able to comprehend
with all the saints what is the breadth and length and height and
depth, and to know the love of Christ which surpasses knowledge,
that you may be filled up to all the fullness of God.

— Ephesians 3:14-19

God, Who "is at work in you, both to will and to work for His good pleasure" (Philippians 2:13), is forming Christ in you and the losses of this realm's perishables are the labor pains which allows Christ to be born in you. A humble vessel, yes, but as a habitation for Christ you are the Father's preference.

Such unfathomable love gives you vision. You pick up your cross, the denial of self-interest, and follow Christ's love for His people. You taste and see that the Lord is good and that He is your treasure regardless of whether you are experiencing a season of abundance or a season of lack. You assent to both loss and gain for the sake of His Kingdom's interests and find that Christ is the treasure in the field; Christ is the pearl of great value.

> *"The kingdom of heaven is like a treasure hidden in the field, which a man found and hid again; and from joy over it he goes and sells all that he has and buys that field. Again, the kingdom of heaven is like a merchant seeking fine pearls, and upon finding one pearl of great value, he went and sold all that he had and bought it."*
>
> — Matthew 13:44-45

I am sure there is many a heart that says: "Ah, but that absolute surrender implies so much!"

Someone says: "Oh, I have passed through so much trial and suffering, and there is so much of the self-life still remaining, and I dare not face the entire giving of it up, because I know it will cause so much trouble and agony."

Alas! alas! that God's children have such thoughts of Him, such cruel thoughts. Oh, I come to you with a message, a fearful and anxious one. God does not ask you to give the perfect surrender in your strength, or by the power of your will; God is willing to work it in you. Do we not read: "It is God that worketh in us, both to will and to do of his good pleasure"? (Philippians 2:13)

And that is what we should seek for—to go on our faces before God until our hearts learn to believe that the everlasting God Himself will come in to turn out what is wrong, to conquer what is evil, and to work what is well-pleasing in His blessed sight.

Look at the men in the Old Testament, like Abraham. Do you think it was by accident that God found that man, the father of the faithful and the Friend of God, and that it was Abraham himself, apart from God, who had such faith and such obedience and such devotion? You know it is not so. God raised him up and prepared him as an instrument for His glory.

Did not God say to Pharaoh: "For this cause have I raised thee up, for to show in thee my power"? (Exodus 9:16) And if God said that of him, will not God say it far more of every child of His?

Oh, I want to encourage you, and I want you to cast away every fear. Come with that feeble desire; and if there is the fear which says: "Oh, my desire is not strong enough, I am not willing for everything that may come, I do not feel bold enough to say I can conquer everything"—I pray you, learn to know and trust your God now. Say: "My God, I am willing that Thou shouldst make me willing." If there is anything holding you back, or any sacrifice you are afraid of making, come to God now, and prove how gracious your God is, and be not afraid that He will command from you what He will not bestow.

God comes and offers to work this absolute surrender in you. All these searchings and hungerings and longings that are in your heart, I tell you they are the drawings of the divine magnet, Christ Jesus. He lived a life of absolute surrender, He has possession of you; He is living in your heart by His Holy Spirit. You have hindered and hindered Him terribly, but He desires to help you to get hold of Him entirely. And He comes and draws you now by His message and words. Will you not come and trust God to work in you that absolute surrender to Himself? Yes, blessed be God, He can do it, and He will do it.

God not only claims it and works it, but God accepts it when we bring it to Him.

— Andrew Murray (1828-1917), *Absolute Surrender*

PART II
BUILDING THE STRUCTURE WITH CHRIST

Once the foundation is laid, it's time to build the functional and aesthetic structure of the church, the Body of Christ.

The function? The serving of God's will.

The aesthetic? The glory of God in earthen vessels.

All building requires materials and sourcing those materials requires the material to be removed from its natural place. Once acquired, the material must be transformed to serve the needs of the structure. God's Kingdom within you operates within this same principle: loss, transformation, serving God's will and finally, glory.

YOU: AT THE CROSSROADS OF AN EXCHANGE

You want the suffering to stop. You're scared. You know that you love God, and yet, your future in His Kingdom has lost its appeal. You pray, you claim, you quote. You repeat your prayers, your claims and your quotes. You get others to pray, to claim, to quote. The suffering doesn't stop. God appears not to care. And after all you've done for Him! Your good behavior has been for nothing.

Or, you believe Satan's lies. You re-visit past hurts to confirm your suspicions: God doesn't love you. Or, you think that God is punishing you. You re-visit your past sins and conclude the tally too great: God is mad at you. It was only a matter of time. Trials and tribulations open the cracks in your foundation and the false structure of your life can't bear the strain; it comes apart.

In the Kingdom of God, the testing of your faith is purposed to expose everything faulty in order to rebuild with Christ. Christ is the only foundation which once laid and built upon will resist leveling-winds, overwhelming-floods and Satan's lies. Though Satan's fiery darts are purposed to overwhelm your standing inside the love of God and Christ's sufficiency, his dark lies are not as powerful as the light of truth. Light always overcomes darkness. You will overcome. The cracks in your faith which allowed lies to penetrate will be filled with Christ: the Way, the Truth, and the Life.

You're there. Your cracks are gaping but you want to be rebuilt. How?

Cracks in your faith require a response. Before you entered the Kingdom of God, you possessed only your carnal nature to meet your needs; your deliverance, your ability to cope, your very happiness was up to your unwise management. Now, as a child of God's Kingdom, you face a fork in the road, another path. You stop and consider the new path. It appears steep and narrow but the promised vista draws you toward its incline.

Still, you hesitate.

Your former life outside of the Kingdom of God had its advantages, you think. The self-determination you knew in your former days is tempting to go back to. Will Satan's offers to go back begin to look attractive? Satan offers:

Immorality (adultery)

Impurity (fornication)

Sensuality (uncleanness)

Idolatry (idol worship)

Sorcery (Satan worship)

Enmities (hatred)

Strife (contentions)

Jealousy (punitive zeal)

Outbursts of anger

Disputes (self-seeking rivalry)

Dissensions (division)

Factions (heresy)

Envying (ill will due to envy)

Drunkenness

Carousing (partying)

And things like these, of which I forewarn you, just as I have forewarned you, that those who practice such things will not inherit the kingdom of God.

— Galatians 5:19-21

Satan has long commanded his demons to tempt the redeemed with their former lusts because when the redeemed choose death over life it puts Christ to an open shame by putting Christ back on the cross and leaving Him there, dead, lifeless.

But bondage to Satan no longer attracts you. You know God loves you in ways you can't yet fathom but His love looks scary at times.

This leaves you in a no-man's land–the Gaza of Kingdom life, the land between faith and independent action. Can you resist the temptation to go back to running your own life?

May I come along-side and assure you that you are only leaving death behind?

May I open your clasped hands and help you let go?

May I help you agree with the Apostle Paul,

> *Brethren, I do not regard myself as having laid hold of it yet; but one thing I do: forgetting what lies behind and reaching forward to what lies ahead, I press on toward the goal for the prize of the upward call of God in Christ Jesus. Let us therefore, as many as are perfect, have this attitude; and if in anything you have a different attitude, God will reveal that also to you; however, let us keep living by that same standard to which we have attained.*

> — Philippians 3:13-16

May I help you not look back? May I help you look forward to:

Your upward call,

Your high calling,

Your perfection?

And in losing all, you will find you have gained true rest, true freedom and true expressions of the Spirit of Christ reigning within:

Love,

Joy,

Peace,

Patience,

Kindness,

Goodness,

Faithfulness,

Gentleness,

And self-control, against such things there is no law. Now those who belong to Christ Jesus have crucified the flesh with its passions and desires

If we live by the Spirit, let us also walk by the Spirit.
— Galatians 5:22-25

Living in the Spirit permits walking in the Spirit.

Walking in the Spirit stems from living in the Spirit.

The fruit of the Spirit isn't under your command. They are not your efforts at good character. When you feel jealous and think, I must not be jealous; I must love, you exert love but your efforts are external like plastic fruit-looking ornaments hung on a tree. Inside, you remain unchanged. Worse, if you believe yourself successful, you become proud. All the while, your natural man remains jealous for jealousy is natural to it. After many failed attempts, you do better to accept that your natural man can only produce jealousy.

The fruit of the Spirit is the expression of Christ living within the redeemed. You abide in the Vine (Christ), you assent and submit to the flow of His living processes, and in due season, you naturally bring about an outward expression of those inner workings. Along the way, your branch is repeatedly pruned of your old nature, often painfully, in order that you produce living fruit for the health of others. Living fruit, rather than leaving you proud, leaves you humbled.

You see the difference between flesh and spirit. Will you choose life over death?

Yes, yes you will.

> For us however, there is a time coming when our spiritual warfare will be finished, our perspective enlarged and our understanding increased. Then we will look back on the experiences through which the Lord led us and be overwhelmed with love and adoration for Him. We will then see that mercy and goodness directed every step. We will see that what we once mistakenly called afflictions and misfortune were in reality blessings without which we would not have grown in faith.
>
> — John Newton (1725-1807)

YOU: ASSENTING TO A KINGDOM EXCHANGE

Kingdom exchanges vary in cost depending on who is paying. For the natural man, the cost is equitably light: asking.

Then He said to me, "It is done. I am the Alpha and the Omega, the beginning and the end. I will give to the one who thirsts from the spring of the water of life without cost."

— Revelation 21:6

Jesus answered and said to her, "If you knew the gift of God, and who it is who says to you, 'Give Me a drink,' you would have asked Him, and He would have given you living water."

— John 4:10

Just asking. No more, no less.

Once you were given a new nature, the old was exposed. You saw that your old nature couldn't meet the requirement of sacrificial, true love (*agape*). The old nature could only be self-centered. It could only love itself.

You press on forgetting what lay behind. The mark of your new calling inside the Kingdom of God bestows fresh, holy appetites which when fed and watered grow and increase in strength. But something surprises you. Contrary to what you imagined, even your "good" strengths are taken away until they bear the mark of the cross. You grieve and are heartbroken. What you thought were talents for you to use for God are revealed as temptations for glorifying self.

Stripped of the temptation, you enter a season of cross-imprinting which so marks your strengths with the face of Christ that *you* disappear. And further, you want to disappear.

"Truly, truly, I say to you, unless a grain of wheat falls into the earth and dies, it remains alone; but if it dies, it bears much fruit. He who loves his life loses it, and he who hates his life in

this world will keep it to life eternal. If anyone serves Me, he
must follow Me; and where I am, there My servant will be also;
if anyone serves Me, the Father will honor him."

—— John 12:24-26

We are dead with Christ, we are buried with Christ, we
are risen with Christ; and there is no real spiritual life in this
world except that which has come to us by the process of death,
burial, and resurrection with Christ. Do you know anything
about this, dear friends?–for if you do not, you know not the
life of God. You know the theory, but do you know the exper-
imental power of this within your own spirit?

—— Charles H. Spurgeon (1834-1892), *Farm Sermons*

PART III
FURNISHING THE STRUCTURE
WITH CHRIST

YOU: EXCHANGING LOSS

The shine is off life. Every day takes on a grey colorlessness. Mornings are difficult. You rise from your bed of grief only when you push yourself and only because you must. Daily responsibilities become a flat, tasteless soup of getting through. You live, but without a will to live. People ask how you're doing. You force a smile and an "okay" to deny them entrance but those closest to you know that you're in a state of unreachable unhappiness. They've tried for weeks, perhaps months, but their well-intended words ricochet off the wall you've raised.

You're unhappy. Worse, you know the truth: once happiness is lost, a hitherto locked door opens and you are shoved into a darkened room where scary possibilities are forever possible. You struggle. You doubt. You ask the questions: "Is God harsh? How could He let this happen?"

Loss.

A person, your health, a material object, a pet, a dream, money, self-respect—you lost it and you miss it. Your happiness was dependent on it. Because of it, you got out of bed, went to work, took care of children, came home and did it all over again the next day.

Loss leaves a painful vacuum which cries to be filled. It's natural to assume relief lies in the happy restoration of the person, place or thing, or at the very least, a replacement. Though you crave safety and control, the temporal world you once trusted in no longer feels safe and secure. Happiness is exposed as transient, fragile, slippery. You can't go back but you don't want to go forward. You stand at a crossroads but neither path holds appeal.

You begin to search for someone alive, a guide, to direct you through your wilderness. Not just anyone will do; they must have certain characteristics. They must be on the other side of an equal or even greater loss and they must be able to smile and say, "I'm better off because of what I went through. You'll be fine too."

You find some; they disappoint. They tell you things you don't want to hear: That they're still sad at times. That, yes, life goes on but you'll always miss what you lost—that it can't be replaced.

You come away uncomforted. You don't want to know that you will never be the same. You don't want to hear that the future won't erase the past.

You don't give up. You dig deeper.

Prayer, impossible in the first rawness of loss, begins again. It's not like the prayer you used to practice. This is desperate, even petulant prayer. You tell God that for you to trust Him, you need answers. This seems to you a fair trade, almost a bargain. But no answer comes.

Hopeful the Word will answer, you tentatively open your Bible. Will you find comfort there or will it only confirm your new, secret suspicion that God is a celestial bully? You read the pages of small, black and red print, the familiar stories of angst and loss, the tears and petitions but then . . . you see something else.

A pattern that you've never before appreciated.

You see that the loss of perishable things gains the sufferer the imperishable. In both the Old and New Testaments you find your guides.

Paul sums up his loss and gain,

> *More than that, I count all things to be loss in view of the surpassing value of knowing Christ Jesus my Lord, for whom I have suffered the loss of all things, and count them but rubbish so that I may gain Christ, and may be found in Him, not having a righteousness of my own derived from the Law, but that which is though faith in Christ, the righteousness which comes from God on the basis of faith, that I may know Him and the power of his resurrection and the fellowship of His sufferings, being conformed*

*to His death; in order that I may attain to the resurrection from
the dead.*

— Philippians 3:8-11

In the wilderness, the desert, your stripping is outside of your control. You can't rejoice. You wanted freedom, not this. And like the people of Israel, you long to go back to Egypt. You're so aware of your hunger and thirst that even slavery looks preferable.

How long will you remain in the desert wilderness? A good question. A better question: How long will it take until I desire the Promised Land more than Egypt?

The answer is known … by God, the merciful God, the just God, the loving God. The God that doesn't measure time in days, weeks, months or years but by fullness. In the Kingdom of God, fullness is judged by spiritual factors and levels you cannot always fathom. But as you wait, you are promised strength to endure and as your overcoming faith increases, you will come to accept that His timing is beyond reproach.

God promises you this: your time in the wilderness is only as long as needed.

*Do you not know? Have you not heard? The Everlasting
God, the LORD, the Creator of the ends of the earth does not
become weary or tired. His understanding is inscrutable.*

*He gives strength to the weary, and to him who lacks
might He increases power.*

*Though youths grow weary and tired, and vigorous young
men stumble badly,*

Yet those who wait for the LORD will gain new strength;
They will mount up with wings like eagles, they will run and not
get tired, they will walk and not become weary.

— Isaiah 40:28-31

Fear not! Loss is the prescriptive paradox where your true relief resides. Loss is the means whereby you become a loss overcomer. In God's Kingdom, loss is your guide to spiritual, and thus eternal, gain.

"These things I have spoken to you, so that in Me you may
have peace. In the world you have tribulation, but take courage;
I have overcome the world."

— John 16:33

Overcoming presupposes something to overcome. True victory lies not in the removal of the loss but in the power you've been given to rise victorious over the weaker power of what you have deemed necessary to your happy state. As light is more powerful than darkness, you too will be given power to rise above the inferior happy state to the joyous state of an overcomer.

Many loss sufferers have gone before you and many will come after. In the Kingdom of God, all join the Apostle Paul and proclaim, "Loss is gain! My loss has been redeemed by a higher sufficiency: My Redeemer!"

I count all things to be loss in view of the surpassing value
of knowing Christ Jesus my Lord.

— Philippians 3:8

For I consider that the sufferings of this present time are not
worthy to be compared with the glory that is to be revealed to us.
— Romans 8:18

Consider it all joy, my brethren, when you encounter
various trials, knowing that the testing of your faith produces
endurance. And let endurance have its perfect result, so that you
may be perfect and complete, lacking in nothing.
— James 1:2-4

Will you assent to God's offerings?

Yes, yes you will. You're not going back; you can't. You lean-in and let-go. You assent to the loss of all things.

Your attachment to the shadows of the Godhead lose power and you find loss has a side-effect: a greater sense of the Kingdom of God. Spiritually, the wilderness of loss becomes to you the land of milk and honey.

You exercise faith in this promise from James and lean-in not away from the pain. There, you find something you didn't expect. What you thought was only to be found at the end of the trial, was found in and through it. Loss becomes gain.

Men ask for exalted summits, as though they were the immediate gift of the Saviour's hand, (but) they are reached by hard and toilsome roads.
— J.H. Jowett, (1863-1923) *The School of Calvary*

YOU: EXCHANGING ALONENESS

An awkward separateness is your new companion. No one understands. Not really. You are in a season of revelation and the discerning of flesh and spirit is becoming a separating sword. You love the revelation but who likes to be misunderstood? Who likes to be alone? Will God give you a friend, a kindred spirit in this valley of tears?

Maybe. Maybe not.

> *When they came to the crowd, a man came up to Jesus,*
> *falling on his knees before Him and saying, "Lord, have mercy on*
> *my son, for he is a lunatic and is very ill; for he often falls into*
> *the fire and often into the water. I brought him to Your disciples,*
> *and they could not cure him." And Jesus answered and said, "You*
> *unbelieving and perverted generation, how long shall I be with*
> *you? How long shall I put up with you? Bring him here to Me."*

And Jesus rebuked him, and the demon came out of him, and the boy was cured at once.

— Matthew 17:14-17

From that time Jesus began to show His disciples that He must go to Jerusalem, and suffer many things from the elders and chief priests and scribes, and be killed, and be raised up on the third day. Peter took Him aside and began to rebuke Him, saying, "God forbid it, Lord! This shall never happen to You."

But He turned and said to Peter, "Get behind Me, Satan! You are a stumbling block to Me; for you are not setting your mind on God's interests, but man's."

Then Jesus said to His disciples, "If anyone wishes to come after Me, he must deny himself, and take up his cross and follow Me. For whoever wishes to save his life will lose it; but whoever loses his life for My sake will find it. For what will it profit a man if he gains the whole world and forfeits his soul? Or what will a man give in exchange for his soul? For the Son of Man is going to come in the glory of His Father with His angels, and will then repay every man according to his deeds."

— Matthew 16:21-27

The narrow way often requires you to suffer, as did Christ, without a friend. The words of loved ones who say more to your comfort than to your consecration leave you uneasy and feeling more alone.

Others you know may speak that your tribulation is related to something you did or didn't do. Listen and hear; humbly take their words before the Lord. If you are led to repentance, rejoice! The

Body of Christ is intended to feed and heal its members. Thank your counselors for their obedience. Further, you will find that when the Lord raises up a particular brother or sister to speak into your season of suffering that they will be an ongoing resource of correction and encouragement.

Like a sword, truth divides the soul and spirit. Will you decide the cost is worth the fellowship you share with Truth Himself?

Will you rejoice even when you feel alone in your suffering?

Yes. Yes, you will.

The narrow way may be uncomfortable but the fellowship your spirit experiences with Christ rises up to drown out the voices of those who would be a stumbling block to what God is building within. Jesus reminds you:

> *"Truly I say to you, there is no one who has left house or*
> *brothers or sisters or mother or father or children or farms, for*
> *My sake and for the gospel's sake, but that he will receive a hun-*
> *dred times as much now in the present age, houses and brothers*
> *and sisters and mothers and children and farms, along with per-*
> *secutions; and in the age to come, eternal life. But many who are*
> *first will be last, and the last, first."*
>
> — Mark 10:29-31

The best piece of furniture I have ever had in my house is the cross of affliction! Adversity is the richest field in all the farm of life. We have never reaped such a harvest from any seed as from that which fell from our hands while tears were falling from our eyes. When we have gone forth weeping, bearing precious seed, we have invariably come again, rejoicing, bringing in our sheaves with us! O sufferer, when your bed grew hard beneath you and your pain was exceedingly great, it may be that your groans and complaints were not altogether those of sorrow, but a measure of rebellion mingled with them! For this, be ashamed and confounded! Confess those rebellions! Acknowledge that your hard thoughts were all founded upon error and ask for grace to be forever at one with your Lord. You who have suffered the loss of property or the loss of beloved friends, you too, perhaps, have thought of God foolishly–remember those thoughts with shame and be all the more eager, at once, to bear willing testimony that the Lord is good and that His mercy endures forever. It is true, however circumstances may look otherwise, that 'the Lord is full of pity, and of tender mercy.' Whatever may or may not be, the Lord must be good! Set your seal to that Truth of God. Hold up your head and your hand as one who can speak well of His name and say, 'I will bless the Lord at all times! His praise shall continually be in my mouth!'

— Charles H. Spurgeon (1834-1892)

a sermon delivered on June 14, 1885

YOU: EXCHANGING FAILURE

You're unhappy. The pattern began when you were young and has repeated too often to be a coincidence. Though you focus, work hard and seek advice, the lacking sum remains the same. You feel the stinging judgments; you don't blame them, you agree–you've failed to be a success materially.

Failure.

It haunts you like the shaggy, stray dog no one wants. Your future used to look bright. Now, the past informs a future without financial success. Others are blessed . . . but not you. No matter what you try–even when you take time to pray and consider, the end is the same.

You find yourself betwixt two opposing minds:

1. Material success isn't important to God.
2. Material success is how God blesses those who are important to Him.

The first is a comfort but the second robs you of that comfort. Around and around you go, from one to the other, longing for absolution from failure's shame.

"Again I say to you, it is easier for a camel to go through the eye of a needle, than for a rich man to enter the kingdom of God."

In the Kingdom of God, material success is not only uncounted, it is considered anathema for its interference. Its temptation to largess prevents the smallness needed to enter into God's Kingdom.

Failure at material success is a true blessing. It enables you to focus on things above and not on things of the earth. The treasures you accumulate there–gold, silver and precious stones–will never leave you. You will enter eternity full of their glory.

Preferring Kingdom Gold Over Gold

Kingdom Gold is the pure truth of the Godhead: Christ. During cataclysmic seasons of your Kingdom life, a shifting occurs, voids open and the Spirit of Truth replaces a lie with Himself. This gold remains a fixed element impervious to change from external influences. No thing and no one can tarnish or change the gold you've been given.

Kingdom Gold attracts, mystifies, humbles and raises up. It is deposited in you to share with God's people and to bring them to maturity. Kingdom Gold shines forth the light, the glorious image of Christ in this world of darkness.

Prior to Truth's impartation, you mined a season of suffering. There, your need for recognition went to the cross and that death broke your need to use Truth to serve yourself. Now, *you* serve Truth.

Cautious and discerning, you sense there are those who will consume Truth and greedily turn to tear and harm you. Though you've been deposited with Truth, it remains His and you must obey the giver of the gold. Impart truth only when God-opened hearts reveal themselves. If you're unsure. Wait, pray, then obey.

Pyrite, a counterfeit gold, is Satan's twist on the truth. It looks similar, is found in similar places and has fooled many. Pyrite is formed from sulfuric acid and iron. It's brittle, unstable, rusts when exposed to moisture, and gives off the characteristic sulfuric odor of the counterfeits Satan fosters in the hearts of man: "immorality, impurity, sensuality, idolatry, sorcery, enmities, strife, jealousy, outbursts of anger, disputes, dissensions, factions, envying, drunkenness, carousing ..." (Galatians 5:19-21a).

Testing and time exposes pyrite. It doesn't remain. Its brittleness can't hold up to life's tests. It doesn't impart glory. It fades over time like all fads do when the winds of doctrine blow in something new but false.

Preferring Kingdom Silver Over Silver

Silver is God's tool of conductivity. It allows His glory to be expressed through you into this realm of darkness. Without it, this world would be a living hell of corruption, exploitation and perversion. Satan's will to steal, kill and destroy would spread unchecked and plague-like throughout the human race. Without silver, there is no true good conducted in the earth.

Some Christ followers live with the anxiety of inadequacy. They sense something inside isn't filled as it should be filled. They find it too easy to become influenced, for good and bad, by external things: People, books, and the media.

You are the Father's child! He longs to give you the best gift: The Holy Spirit (Luke 11:13).

Through the empowering baptism of fire, you will not only be reminded of all truth, you will gain the discernment necessary to apply it properly. Also, the power to endure long trials will light your lamp with all the light you will need until the Bridegroom arrives to receive His church.

Without the purifying baptism of fire, a believer can know truth but lack the guiding discernment necessary to apply it properly. Also, endurance for long trials is impossible because it is dependent; it doesn't come from within. Christ followers without this second baptism live with the continual fear that their faith is directly related to their present company or influence. This insecure state does not serve over time; the wait for the Bridegroom is long and difficult and borrowed oil will run out in times of trial.

It also does not serve God's purposes for you, a conductor of glory, to foster other's dependency on you. Due to your wind-like qualities, your ministry to the Body of Christ strength-tests foundations, exposes weaknesses, elicits repentance and then, like the wind, moves on–purposely cutting unhealthy cords of dependent flesh.

Silver doesn't allow *you* to perform God's Kingdom ministry; silver allows God to conduct His ministry *through* you. Contrary to your best attempts at ministry using your own power, might or imagination, silver is deposited when you sit at His feet in humble acceptance of His exhortation, "Apart from Me, you can do nothing." Like conducting branches on the vine, you first receive the flow and your fruit is the natural expression of that conductivity.

Preferring Kingdom Precious Stones Over Precious Stones

Precious stones are formed when super-heated mineral ores go through the filtering process of the earth's crust and deposit their unique crystals in pockets. Color is determined by the unique characteristics of each mineral or combination of minerals.

If you find something you think is a precious stone, do you hold it up to the light and enjoy the color the light magnifies? Do you peer inside the crystal to explore the depths of it's color? Do you call over others to share your delight? Do you wonder, "Is it real? Is it worth anything?"

How can you know for sure?

Test and see.

Precious stones hold up to tests for hardness, color, and ability to magnify light.

As living temples of God, we are constructed of building materials which allow the structure to stand firm on the foundation which is Christ. This practical structure houses not only God's glory it also houses the functions which recognize His preeminence and precious stones are the deposits within God's people that display particular aspects of His glory.

> *He who descended is himself also He who ascended far above all the heavens, so that He might fill all things. And He gave some as apostles, and some as prophets, and some as evangelists, and some as pastors and teachers, for the equipping of the saints for the work of service, to the building up of the body of Christ, until we all attain to the unity of the faith, and of the knowledge of the son of God, to a mature man, to the measure of the stature which belongs to the fullness of Christ. As a result, we are no longer children, tossed here and there by waves and carried about by every wind of doctrine, by the trickery of men, by craftiness in deceitful scheming, but speaking the truth in love, we are to grow up in all aspects into Him who is the head, even Christ, from whom the whole body, being fitted and held together by what every joint supplies, according to the proper working of each individual part, causes the growth of the body for the building up of itself in love.*
>
> — Ephesians 4:10-16

No one can, nor is any one person meant to house all the colors which make up God's glory. The entire Body of Christ, expressing glory through our earthly vessels are united in faith, in

the knowledge of the Son of God and in process of becoming the
fullness of Christ.

Again, the Apostle Paul shares this truth in terms of God's
deposit of gifts. To the church at Corinth he writes:

> *Now you are Christ's body, and individually members of*
> *it. And God has appointed in the church, first apostles, second*
> *prophets, third teachers, then miracles, then gifts of healings,*
> *helps, administrations, various kinds of tongues.*
>
> *All are not apostles, are they? All are not prophets, are they?*
> *All are not teachers, are they? All are not workers of miracles, are*
> *they? All do not have gifts of healings, do they? All do not speak*
> *with tongues, do they? All do not interpret, do they? But earnestly*
> *desire the greater gifts. And I show you a still more excellent way.*
> —1 Corinthians 12:27-31

The glory of the Body of Christ is glorious; the pure expression
of light. All colors of the spectrum coming together–a city on a
hill: ZION.

Gold, silver and precious stones. Will you value their spiritual
worth over that of material success?

Yes. Yes, you will.

In seeking the One you love above all else, you find everything
truly lovable. When that glorious day comes and you are fitted with
the crown awaiting you, it will be only fitting that you reach up,
remove it, and lay it at Christ's feet (Revelation 4:10).

> If the world were mine and all its store,
> And were it of crystal gold;
> Could I reign on its throne for evermore

From the ancient days of old,

An empress noble and fair as day,

O gladly might it be,

That I might cast it all away;

Christ, only Christ for me.

For Christ my Lord my spirit longs,

For Christ, my Saviour dear;

The joy and sweetness of my songs

The whilst I wander here–

O Lord, my spirit fain would flee

From the lonely desert away to Thee.

> — Emma Frances Bevan (1827-1909), *The Exchange*

YOU: EXCHANGING REJECTION

You're hurting. It's a disabling kind of pain wrapped in anger and regret. You can't eat. Or, you eat too much attempting to push the pain down with each swallow. Sleep comes in snatches. Breathing is a chore demanding your focus. Your thoughts race like a panicked horse or slow like the drip, drip of water torture causing you to obsess over past events.

You feel immobilized. Moving forward is impossible–your very self-concept and future happiness were dependent on the love and acceptance you've lost.

You know a few things about love even if you don't understand it. You know you need it. You know that other people need it. You know that love feels good. So good, in fact, that you are willing to go to great lengths to get it.

You also know what you don't know about love. You don't know how to guarantee yourself a limitless supply and, conversely, you yourself love with limits. You conclude you don't know how to love others but you also don't know how to live without others' love.

You settled for temporal expressions. But, at your core, you were scared; you understood the risks inherent to imperfect, human love. You knew that your spouse could find someone else to love. You knew your friend could do the same. You knew children could ignore their parents. Or maybe you worried that you'd be the one to lose love for your spouse, your friend, your child.

Now, you're there. The days pile up without relief. Finally, while crying out to God for His mind in the matter, you gain some light to guide you down the narrow blade separating soul and spirit. You see that regaining the tenuous love you've lost isn't going to give you lasting or true relief. The blade can now reveal the astounding truth: the imperfect love of this realm is purposed to leave you hungry for the One Who *is* love.

On earth, you will long for and experience different types of love. The Greeks have four words for love: *Agape, Eros, Storge* and *Philia.*

Eros–the sensual love between two people.

Storge–the protective love between parent and child.

Philia–the mutual-satisfaction love between friends.

Eros, Philia and *Storge* are imperfect and will pass away. Driven, at times compulsively by self-interest, you know they are not true love but you are driven by them and towards them as if your life depended on it. It doesn't.

Each of these types of love is intended to serve this temporary realm for better or worse and will, intentionally, leave you longing for *Agape.* Their painful loss, redeemed by the One Who is perfect Love Himself, allows you to know true love–Himself. He is standing at the ready, offering you freedom from the enslaving need to be loved by those unable.

Are you ready for a love which never passes away?

Yes, yes you are.

Emptied and ready to be filled, you sit like Mary at His feet or like John against His breast eating and drinking of Him. Your eyes brim with the overflow of a wholly satisfying love from Christ Who becomes the one thing needful.

Once you are released from bondage of love's temporal expressions, *agape* is expressed through you in the gift of your calling. This love is different; it's no longer about you. You're free.

> It is in the fires of suffering that God purifies His saints
> and brings them to the highest things.
> — E. M. Bounds (1835-1913), *Essentials of Prayer*

YOU: EXCHANGING CONFUSION AND UNCERTAINTY

You are standing on the border of something new and scary.
Behind you lies the cushioned nursery where your requests often
moved His hand in miraculous and surprising ways making you feel
favored and protected. Now, your future stretches like a wilderness
full of the unknown. One thing is sure–you don't like it and your

anguish makes you desperate enough to complain like a petulant and unseeing two-year-old, "God, why have you abandoned me?"

Maturing in Christ requires progressive stages and you can't go back to the nursery. You've outgrown it. A new stage has begun and it begins with a wilderness fasting from self-centered love. It's time for you to love your Father's Kingdom and empathize with the mind of Christ above your kingdom and your mind.

You may recall a specific prayer you prayed. It sprang from your spirit and rang like church bells in and through you. It went something like, "Lord, I want to know You. Nothing else but You. I give everything to know You. Nothing else but You." You may have raised your hands in surrender. Your spirit danced with knowing assent. Your mind retaliated with consequent probabilities but you didn't care; your spirit won. Connection with the lover of your soul triumphed over all and your spirit sung in spirit and in truth.

You couldn't appreciate back then that to fully know God, in spirit and in truth, it would require your personal powerlessness.

In this realm, power moves the temporal to work man's will. In the Kingdom of God, power brings men's hearts under the Lordship of Christ. "We are destroying speculations and every lofty thing raised up against the knowledge of God, and we are taking every thought captive to the obedience of Christ" (2 Corinthians 10:5).

In the temporal, power moves wheat to become bread. In the Kingdom of God, Christ is our bread. In the temporal, material possession is power. In the Kingdom of God, Christ is our only possession. In the temporal, signs and wonders prove God's faithfulness. In the Kingdom of God, Christ is proof enough of God's faithfulness.

While in the wilderness, Christ couldn't be tempted by Satan's temporal offers of bread, power and protection. Likewise, Satan cannot tempt you with that which will pass away. Your heart belongs to Christ and He has crushed the power of Satan's deadly offers. Furthermore, Christ surpasses the temporal–exchanging death for abundant life.

> *"Truly, truly, I say to you, I am the door of the sheep. All who came before Me are thieves and robbers, but the sheep did not hear them. I am the door; if anyone enters through Me, he will be saved, and will go in and out and find pasture. The thief comes only to steal and kill and destroy; I came that they may have life, and have it abundantly."*
>
> — John 10:7-10

Will you exchange the comfort of certainty for trust in God? Yes, yes you will.

> *As an example, brethren, of suffering and patience, take the prophets who spoke in the name of the Lord. We count those blessed who endured. You have heard of the endurance of Job and have seen the outcome of the Lord's dealings that the Lord is full of compassion and is merciful.*
>
> — James 5:10-11

Trust is the new ground you own. Gratefully, you look toward the future with the words of a seeing Joseph for inspiration,

*"God sent me before you to preserve for you a remnant in
the earth, and to keep you alive by a great deliverance. Now,
therefore, it was not you who sent me here, but God; and He has
made me a father to Pharaoh and lord of all his household and
ruler over all the land of Egypt."*

— Genesis 45:7-8

Like Joseph, what you thought was uncertainty and confusion
will be exchanged: your coat of many colors exchanged for fine
linen, a ring and a gold chain. Your betrayal, slavery and captivity
has been exchanged for chariot access to the whole land of Egypt.
Your powerlessness has been redeemed by power equal to Pharaoh.

He gives abundantly but not as you expect.

*"Peace I leave with you; My peace I give to you; not as the
world gives do I give to you. Do not let your heart be troubled,
nor let it be fearful. You heard that I said to you, 'I go away, and
I will come to you.' If you loved Me, you would have rejoiced
because I go to the Father, for the Father is greater than I. Now
I have told you before it happens, so that when it happens, you
may believe. I will not speak much more with you, for the ruler
of the world is coming, and he has nothing in Me; but so that the
world may know that I love the Father, I do exactly as the Father
commanded Me."*

— John 14:27-31

In 1923 I was invited to preach in a certain city. I took a
small boat that was sailing up the Ming River. I noticed that
the boat was frequently dragging itself against the river bed,
for the water was shallow and the bottom of the river was

rugged. Sometimes the boatmen had to pull the boat by ropes up the river. In my prayer I suddenly recalled this incident. I said, 'God it is easy for You to remove these rocks. How nice it would be for the boat to sail with adequate water underneath it if You simply remove these rocks.' I read again 2 Corinthians 12, where I found this to be precisely Paul's prayer. The water was shallow and the rocks protruded sharply up from the river bed. Hence Paul was praying, 'O God, would that You might remove these rocks that my boat may sail in the water.' To which God answered, 'I will not remove these rocks, but I will cause the water to rise. As the water rises, the boat can easily sail through.' This is God's doing.

> — Watchman Nee (1903-1972),
> *Christ, The Sum of All Spiritual Things*

YOU: EXCHANGING SICKNESS, DISEASE AND DISABILITY

You're not getting well. Prayers have been said, repeated and hands laid upon, and yet you remain sick and disabled. Doctors have been consulted, medications and therapies prescribed and followed, and still, you suffer. Fear becomes your constant companion. The dark tidal wave of hopelessness threatens to knock you down and smother you.

Your loved ones compound your suffering. The worry which clouds their eyes is another burden you must carry. Kind friends who step in to relieve you of day to day tasks leave you both grateful and shamed at your inability. Conversely, if you have young children, they may seem unaffected. They're too noisy, too unruly and often unhelpful. Adult children care better but assisting you is time away from their own responsibilities which leaves you uneasy.

You're forced to learn to live with your new companion: pain. Its needs for accommodation drown out everyone else's needs, including your own.

Does your physical malady mean something, you wonder? Is the Lord speaking through it?

Yes, He is.

Are you willing to listen, and hear?

Yes, yes you are.

Clutching 2 Corinthians Chapter 4, you lean-in and listen to your King who has allowed the physical to speak of the spiritual.

You may hear:

Pain, disease and disability are allowed to showcase in the heavenly realms your devotion to the One your soul loves above all. Your praise of God in the midst of your pain puts Satan on notice. Your praise dismisses his accusations with the true saying, "You have gained permission to afflict me but you cannot separate me from the love of God which is in Christ Jesus, my Lord."

The LORD said to Satan, "Have you considered My servant
Job? For there is no one like him on the earth, a blameless and
upright man, fearing God and turning away from evil." Then
Satan answered the LORD, "Does Job fear God for nothing?

Have You not made a hedge about him and his house and all

that he has, on every side? You have blessed the work of his hands,

and his possessions have increased in the land. But put forth Your

hand now and touch all that he has; he will surely curse You to

Your face." Then the LORD said to Satan, "Behold, all that he

has is in your power, only do not put forth your hand on him."

So Satan departed from the presence of the LORD.

— Job 1:8-12

Or, you may hear:

Pain, disease and disability are allowed in answer to your prayer for humility. Each effectively protect the Kingdom of God's interests from getting mixed-up with your personal ego's interests.

Because of the surpassing greatness of the revelations, for

this reason, to keep me from exalting myself, there was given me

a thorn in the flesh, a messenger of Satan to torment me—to keep

me from exalting myself!

— 2 Corinthians 12:7

Your mortal body is a temporary house for God's Kingdom on this earth. His purposes for certain servants will allow them to experience great revelations which can tempt them to fall into pride. Physical maladies, like Paul's, serve to separate flesh from spirit with sacred efficiency.

Also for God's servants is the problem of focus. For God's purposes to have the preeminence they require, maladies often allow for a season of reflection and repentance. After this work is done God's Kingdom interests reign supreme above all else on earth. You will restructure your days in order that the Lord becomes first in thought and deed.

In both cases, your new found humility springs forth naturally in fewer words spoken, fewer plans made, and all plans submitted to God for approval.

> *All discipline for the moment seems not to be joyful, but sorrowful; yet to those who have been trained by it, afterwards it yields the peaceful fruit of righteousness. Therefore, strengthen the hands that are weak and the knees that are feeble, and make straight paths for your feet, so that the limb which is lame may not be put out of joint, but rather be healed.*
>
> — Hebrews 12:11-13

Or, you may hear:

Pain, disease and disability are allowed to give you insight into your personal spiritual pain and disease which has hampered you in being the source of spiritual health for others. Pray for revelation. Bring your ailment to the Body of Christ, confess and have prayer for healing.

> *Is anyone among you suffering? Then he must pray. Is anyone cheerful? He is to sing praises. Is anyone among you sick? Then he must call for the elders of the church and they are to pray over him, anointing him with oil in the name of the Lord; and the prayer offered in faith will restore the one who is sick, and the Lord will raise him up, and if he has committed sins, they will be forgiven him. Therefore, confess your sins to one another, and pray for one another so that you may be healed.*
>
> — James 5:13-16

Or, you may hear:

Pain and disease are allowed to give you an intercessor's share in the sufferings of Christ. Paul's eye disease was allowed for his humbling but it also gave him intercession on behalf of the Jews' inability to recognize the Messiah. So too, your disease rightly mirrors a spiritual disease that the Lord desires you to mourn over for the Body of Christ's sake. Take this mantle seriously and responsibly. The intercession you will be given will flow from you naturally and break spiritual bondages.

> *Now I rejoice in my sufferings for your sake, and in my flesh I do my share on behalf of His body, which is the church, in filling up what is lacking in Christ's afflictions. Of this church I was made a minister according to the stewardship from God bestowed on me for your benefit, so that I might fully carry out the preaching of the word of God, that is, the mystery which has been hidden from the past ages and generations, but has now been manifested to His saints, to whom God willed to make known what is the riches of the glory of this mystery among the Gentiles, which is Christ in you, the hope of glory. We proclaim Him, admonishing every man and teaching every man with all wisdom, so that we may present every man complete in Christ. For this purpose also I labor, striving according to His power, which mightily works within me.*
>
> — Colossians 1:24-29

In each of the four examples your pain and disease, or disability, offer you an exchange:

Immaturity for maturity

Fear for trust

Complaint for praise

Pride for humility

Pain for the fellowship of Christ's sufferings

Disease for your own spiritual health or the spiritual health
of the Body of Christ

Suffering for a share in Christ's glory

I hear that Christ hath been so kind as to visit you with
sickness. He would have more service of you. He is your loving
husband, and would draw you into the bonds of a sweeter love.
Look at your companionship! 'Rejoice,' inasmuch as the Lord
is with you in unceasing fellowship.

— Samuel Rutherford (1600-1661)
from a letter to Lady Forrest

YOU: EXCHANGING CAPTIVITY

You are under the control of a power greater than your own. Day after day, month after month, or year after year, you must submit to your captor's whims. Your will is usurped by their evil intentions leaving you helpless and full of fear. You may cry and rage but it's to no avail; your will, self-determination, and future are strangled with no relief in sight.

Captivity.

Unlike the deadly captivity to sin, periods of powerlessness against an earthly power have been used by God throughout time to release His people into new consecrations. Your prayers for release go unanswered because your captivity is purposed to set you and others free. In Christ, you live in true freedom, regardless of your circumstances.

Your season of powerlessness, in time, becomes a sanctuary where your eyes are opened to the captivity of your former days. The repentances you offer, the revelations you are given, and your ascents to greater heights of sanctification are worth the deprivations and humiliations you endure. Each allows your perception of the love of Christ for others to deepen and to heighten your understanding of His Kingdom purposes for His beloved.

Captivity purifies you to be free to love the captives of sin with the love of Christ.

Will you, as Christ did, assent to the exchange of your freedom for the freedom of others?

Yes. Yes, you will.

No earthly power can come against you without God's permission; Christ wasn't a victim nor are you a victim.

> *Jesus answered, "You would have no authority over Me,*
> *unless it had been given you from above; for this reason he who*
> *delivered Me to you has the greater sin."*
>
> — John 19:11

During captivity, you enjoy a spiritual honeymoon with the mind of Christ. You find Christ's mercy for your captors in spite of their mercilessness. You find Christ's love for your captors in spite of their hate. And for the sake of your brethren's freedom, you find the laying down of your life natural and proper.

One great lesson arose from all the beatings, tortures, and butchery of the Communists: that the spirit is master of the body. We felt the torture, but it often seemed as something distant and far removed from the spirit which was lost in the glory of Christ and His presence with us. When we were given one slice of bread a week and dirty soup every day, we decided we would faithfully tithe even then. Every tenth week we took the slice of bread and gave it to weaker brethren as our tithe to the Master. I don't feel frustrated to have lost many years in prison. I have seen beautiful things. I myself have been among the weak and insignificant ones in prison, but have had the privilege to be in the same jail with great saints, heroes of faith who equaled the Christians of the first centuries. They went gladly to die for Christ. The spiritual beauty of such saints and heroes of faith can never be described. The things that I say here are not exceptional. The supernatural things have become natural to Christians in the Underground Church who have returned to their first love.

— Richard Wurmbrand (1909-2001), *Tortured For Christ*

YOU: EXCHANGING POVERTY

Hunger, weakness and sorrow fill your days. You remember God's promises of blessing and feel He has failed and forsaken you. You compare your lack to other's surplus and moan at the discrepancy. Your hunger becomes more than physical and emotional. Now, it's spiritual. The poison of faithlessness, spins you into depression. You cry out to God, "Haven't I been a good Christian? Will I praise you from a bitter grave?"

God answers,

> *"I am the bread of Life."*
>
> *"For My flesh is true food, and My blood is true drink. He who eats My flesh and drinks My blood abides in Me, and I in him."*
>
> *"Do not work for the food which perishes, but for the food which endures to eternal life, which the Son of Man will give to you, for on Him the Father, God, has set His seal."*
>
> — John 6:35, John 6:55-56, John 6:27

"Do not worry then, saying, 'What will we eat?' or 'What will we drink?' or 'What will we wear for clothing?' For the Gentiles eagerly seek all these things; for your heavenly Father knows that you need all these things. But seek first His kingdom and His righteousness, and all these things will be added to you."

— Matthew 6:31-33

Christ is calling you to a new overcoming. There, God's will becomes your meat and drink. His Kingdom work feeds and sustains you in ways beyond this realm. Bodily needs serve to heighten your longing for more of the mind of Christ. Your body becomes a living sacrifice upon the altar of His Kingdom.

Will you assent to the exchange of physical longings for spiritual ones? Will you allow what is true poverty–spiritual death–to break your heart for the truly hungry?

Will you, like Paul, assent to fastings often?

Yes, yes you will.

Like the deer pants for the water, your soul longs for God more than earthly food.

It is not a question of our blessing or our enjoyment; it is a question of God's testimony, a question of the Church, of the coming of Christ, of the coming of the Kingdom of God upon earth, of the solving of this world's need–the curing of its agony. That is why God would seek to do a fresh work, a work of thorough emptying, in order that He might do a work of glorious filling.

— John Wright Follette (1883-1966)

YOU: EXCHANGING PERSECUTION

They are actively against you. Their presence makes you feel insecure, burdened and robbed of safety and respect. They have words and possibly weapons, both to harm you. It is very personal and you feel it very personally. Your ego races to shore up your defense but though you express your justifications, nothing changes; you are hated without a cause.

Enemies.

It seems incongruous for you, a Christian, to have an enemy; it presupposes you are guilty of an offense. You *are* guilty. Just as Christ was a stumbling block, a rock of offense, so are all of His followers. You have made a choice to stand for a gospel which offends those in darkness. Darkness and light cannot share real estate. The weaker darkness must yield to light and this offends darkness.

> *It is the LORD of hosts whom you should regard as holy.*
> *And He shall be your fear, And He shall be your dread.*
> *Then He shall become a sanctuary; But to both the houses*
> *of Israel, a stone to strike and a rock to stumble over, And a snare*
> *and a trap for the inhabitants of Jerusalem.*
> *Many will stumble over them, Then they will fall and be*
> *broken; They will even be snared and caught.*

— Isaiah 8:13-15

Christ knew you would find the treatment you suffer by the hands of your enemies unjust and to preempt your confusion He forewarned you:

> *"But before all these things, they will lay their hands on*
> *you and will persecute you, delivering you to the synagogues and*
> *prisons, bringing you before kings and governors for My name's*
> *sake. It will lead to an opportunity for your testimony. So make*
> *up your minds not to prepare beforehand to defend yourselves; for*
> *I will give you utterance and wisdom which none of your oppo-*
> *nents will be able to resist or refute. But you will be betrayed even*
> *by parents and brothers and relatives and friends, and they will*
> *put some of you to death, and you will be hated by all because of*

My name. Yet not a hair of your head will perish. By your endurance you will gain your lives."

— Luke 21:12-19

Your enemies serve to gain ground for the Kingdom of God. Your persecution advances the gospel to places hitherto unreached. Christ promises to fill you with irrefutable words and wisdom which will serve to further His mission through His followers:

"THE SPIRIT OF THE LORD IS UPON ME, BE-CAUSE HE ANOINTED ME TO PREACH THE GOSPEL TO THE POOR. HE HAS SENT ME TO PROCLAIM RE-LEASE TO THE CAPTIVES, AND RECOVERY OF SIGHT TO THE BLIND, TO SET FREE THOSE WHO ARE OP-PRESSED, TO PROCLAIM THE FAVORABLE YEAR OF THE LORD."

— Luke 4:18-19

And though you suffer painful relationship losses, Christ promises that your Kingdom personhood has not been disrespected or diminished. Your every hair is numbered–even those which fall.

Furthermore, once you grasp the Kingdom exchange rate for the slap to your face, the theft of your coat or the loss of your freedom you will see that your offer of double what is sought is true gain.

"You have heard that it was said, 'AN EYE FOR AN EYE, AND A TOOTH FOR A TOOTH.' But I say to you, do not resist an evil person; but whoever slaps you on your right cheek, turn the other to him also. If anyone wants to sue you and take your shirt, let him have your coat also. Whoever forces you to go

one mile, go with him two. Give to him who asks of you, and do
not turn away from him who wants to borrow from you.

"You have heard that it was said, 'YOU SHALL LOVE
YOUR NEIGHBOR and hate your enemy.' But I say to you,
love your enemies and pray for those who persecute you, so that
you may be sons of your Father who is in heaven; for He causes
His sun to rise on the evil and the good, and sends rain on the
righteous and the unrighteous. For if you love those who love you,
what reward do you have? Do not even the tax collectors do the
same? If you greet only your brothers, what more are you doing
than others? Do not even the Gentiles do the same? Therefore you
are to be perfect, as your heavenly Father is perfect."

— Matthew 5:38-48

What was unthinkable when you were outside of the Kingdom of God is now commanded of you. You are the earthly expression of your heavenly Father.

Can you love those who persecute you?

Yes, yes you can.

The same Christ who endured, blessed and prayed for His enemies, "Father forgive them for they know not what they do," stirs you to greater capacities and expressions of His love. Now, you too endure your enemies. Now, you too bless your enemies. And now, you too pray for your enemies, "Father forgive them for they know not what they do."

We ought always to give thanks to God for you, brethren,
as is only fitting, because your faith is greatly enlarged, and the
love of each one of you toward one another grows ever greater;

therefore, we ourselves speak proudly of you among the churches of God for your perseverance and faith in the midst of all your persecutions and afflictions which you endure. This is a plain indication of God's righteous judgment so that you will be considered worthy of the kingdom of God, for which indeed you are suffering.

— 2 Thessalonians 1:3-5

We love others, we love everybody, we love our enemies, because He first loved us... And that is how the love of God melts down the unlovely heart in man, and begets in him the new creature, who is patient and humble and gentle and unselfish.

— Henry Drummond (1851-1897)
The Greatest Thing in the World

YOU: EXCHANGING IMPORTUNITY

It's not happening. Time stretches into the future with no relief in sight. At first, your prayers were strong with hopeful, if assumptive, expectation. Then, your prayers became begging for the good end you desired. Now, your prayers are rote and vacant of desire—not really prayers at all.

During long periods of importunity, Satan speaks into these weaknesses you yet have in your perceptions about God:

God doesn't care. God doesn't love me. Depending on your previous experience in wars against Satan's vile roaring, you will be vulnerable or mighty. In either case, this time of waiting and wrestling against Satan's lies is vital to gain the experience needed for future ascents to higher places in God's Kingdom.

After you have suffered for a little while, the God of all
grace, who called you to His eternal glory in Christ, will Himself
perfect, confirm, strengthen and establish you.

— 1 Peter 5:10

Waiting is vital for you to learn the proper use of your weapons; you are equipped but untrained.

We are destroying speculations and every lofty thing raised
up against the knowledge of God, and we are taking every
thought captive to the obedience of Christ ...

— 2 Corinthians 10:5

When Satan pulled a promise from scripture to tempt Jesus in the wilderness, Jesus answered with higher principle from scripture. The higher word for your circumstance will come through revelation. It will suit higher principles than physical ease or physical comfort. This kind of promise will not do harm to you or others.

If you've been given revelation, you've been given a living promise. Memorize your promise and study others who were given promises. Jacob's Joseph was given prophetic dreams which appeared to suffer defeat but the detours and delays which made Joseph despair were, in the end, neither.

Living promises require you to remain secure in the faithfulness of God and to live as though the outcome is finished; as though it is seen even though it is yet unseen.

In addition, you will find comfort knowing that promises are purposely given by God when long seasons of waiting will be required. Labor to rest in faith! Beware of:

Satan's, "Hath God said?"

Your efforts to help God along.

Pressure from others to help God along.

Each spring from doubt and impatience. Each are tacit expressions of distrust. Each lead to Ishmaels, and Ishmael's offspring born of a lack of faith, bring universal grief.

> *Finally, be strong in the Lord and in the strength of His might. Put on the full armor of God, so that you will be able to stand firm against the schemes of the devil. For our struggle is not against flesh and blood, but against the rulers, against the powers, against the world forces of this darkness, against the spiritual forces of wickedness in the heavenly places. Therefore, take up the full armor of God, so that you will be able having girded your loins with truth, to resist in the evil day, and having done everything, to stand firm. Stand firm therefore, and having put on the breastplate of righteousness, and having shod your feet with the preparation of the gospel of peace; in addition to all, taking up the shield of faith with which you will be able to extinguish all the flaming arrows of the evil one. And take the helmet of salvation, and the sword of the Spirit, which is the word of God. With all prayer and petition pray at all times in the Spirit, and with this in view, be on the alert with all perseverance and petition for all the saints.*
>
> — Ephesians 6:10-18

If you don't know God's will, your battle is done in prayer for discernment. But these prayers are not the demanding, willful pleas of a toddler. Your prayers may be plaintive but they are for revelation of your Heavenly Father's heart toward the matter. You long to partner with Him in binding and releasing in the Kingdom.

In both the embrace of God's will and God's heart, your dry desert of waiting becomes an oasis of spiritual provision. Your sense of God's presence is heightened and like the scared Elijah you are fed His love in surprising ways greatly enlarging your faith.

> *Bless our God, O peoples, and sound His praise abroad,*
> *Who keeps us in life and does not allow our feet to slip. For You*
> *have tried us, O God; You have refined us as silver is refined. You*
> *brought us into the net; You laid an oppressive burden upon our*
> *loins. You made men ride over our heads; we went through fire*
> *and through water, yet You brought us out into a place of abun*
> *dance.*
>
> — Psalm 66:8-12 (format altered)

Will you assent to the higher value in God's Kingdom? Even when the exercising of your faith is stretching you beyond your capacity?

Yes, yes you will.

Why? Because faith is the basis of your life in Christ. Your entrance into the Kingdom of God required faith and your maturing in the Kingdom requires no less. Faith displays trust which is our holy love language toward God.

> Could it be that He is only waiting there to see
> if I will learn to love the dreams
> that He has dreamed for me.
>
> — Twila Paris (1958-   ), *I Will Listen*

YOU: EXCHANGING SPIRITUAL LACK

You live with the longing for more spiritual revelation. Your lack, both in comparison with others and the personal longing you hold within, leaves you feeling subpar. You wonder, *Is there something wrong with me? Did I mess up? Does God love others more than me?*

Spiritual lack.

It haunts and robs you of your joy. It affects your spiritual growth in the Kingdom because you deliberately give less of your life to God to communicate your displeasure in His personal attention.

Coveting more of God is not equal to submitting to the more God wills for you. Coveting begs for an addition to what you currently experience and comes from a lack of understanding of homeostasis, balance. As Christ displayed in the physical realm, so in the Kingdom of God: health is a balance between need and consumption. An imbalance of either cannot be sustained over the long-term and affects the health of the Body of Christ. Though wanting more appears the goal of spirituality, experience teaches you two principles governing how God gives:

You must lose to gain.

Comparing yourself to others is not wise.

> *Now large crowds were going along with Him; and He turned and said to them, "If anyone comes to Me, and does not hate his own father and mother and wife and children and brothers and sisters, yes, and even his own life, he cannot be My disciple. Whoever does not carry his own cross and come after Me cannot be My disciple. For which one of you, when he wants to build a tower, does not first sit down and calculate the cost to see if he has enough to complete it? Otherwise, when he has laid a foundation and is not able to finish, all who observe it begin to ridicule him, saying, 'This man began to build and was not able to finish.' Or what king, when he sets out to meet another king in battle, will not first sit down and consider whether he is strong enough with ten thousand men to encounter the one coming against him with twenty thousand? Or else, while the other is still far away, he sends a delegation and asks for terms of peace. So then, none of you can be My disciple who does not give up all his own possessions."*
>
> — Luke 14:25-33

> *For we are not bold to class or compare ourselves with some of those who commend themselves; but when they measure themselves by themselves and compare themselves with themselves, they are without understanding. But we will not boast beyond our*

measure, but within the measure of the sphere which God appor-
tioned to us as a measure, to reach even as far as you. For we are
not overextending ourselves, as if we did not reach to you, for we
were the first to come even as far as you in the gospel of Christ;
not boasting beyond our measure, that is, in other men's labors,
but with the hope that as your faith grows, we will be, within
our sphere, enlarged even more by you, so as to preach the gospel
even to the regions beyond you, and not to boast in what has been
accomplished in the sphere of another. But HE WHO BOASTS
IS TO BOAST IN THE LORD. For it is not he who commends
himself that is approved, but he whom the Lord commends.

— 2 Corinthians 10:12-18

The "more" you seek for requires you becoming less. Are you jumping at the offering? Will you go away sad? Will you find the hundred-fold He promises in this life and in the life to come an exchange rate worthy of becoming last, of becoming a servant, of picking up your cross of self-denial to follow Him?

Desiring more than the measure you've been given negates the sacredness of your calling. Will you live fully in what you've been given and not covet what others have been given?

Yes. Yes, you will.

You count the cost and agree to the exchange. You actively submit to the offering of more, knowing the cost is a giving over of personal ground to God's ownership. You suffer the loss with faith in the promise that what may be loss in this realm is gain in the Kingdom of God.

Christ knows the cost of God's Kingdom–He laid down His life to establish a people filled with His glory and He stands at the right hand of God making intercession for you, His beloved.

But now I come to You; and these things I speak in the world so that they may have My joy made full in themselves. I have given them Your word; and the world has hated them, because they are not of the world, even as I am not of the world. I do not ask You to take them out of the world, but to keep them from the evil one. They are not of the world, even as I am not of the world. Sanctify them in the truth; Your word is truth. As You sent Me into the world, I also have sent them into the world. For their sakes I sanctify Myself, that they themselves also may be sanctified in truth.

— John 17:13-19

There are two ways of getting out of a trial. One is simply to try to get rid of the trial, and be thankful when it is over. The other is to recognize the trial as a challenge from God to claim a larger blessing than we have ever had, and to hail it with delight as an opportunity of obtaining a larger measure of divine grace.

— A. B. Simpson (1843-1919)

You: Exchanging Betrayal

You're stunned; you didn't see the blow coming. It came from a trusted business partner, friend, sweetheart, spouse, sister, brother, son, or daughter–all to better their position at your expense.

Betrayal.

Like a knife piercing your core, your pain is both physical and emotional. Your mind races with both the injustice and your self-justifications. Sleep evades you. Your sense of peace is stripped away by imaginations of retaliation.

For a while, you determine to have purer responses, but your sense of justice overruns your good intentions, leaving you rudderless before the storm, powerless to return to your former equanimity.

Perfect. You've been given the opportunity for a Kingdom exchange beyond compare.

Betrayal serves like nothing else to facilitate the divine purposes found in the fellowship of Christ's sufferings: *agape*. You cannot know the full measure of the love of Christ until you've suffered betrayal.

Hearing Christ is difficult over the loudness of injustice, but when you are able, you will hear Christ inviting you to bear your betrayer's shame.

Betrayal is sourced in shame.

Shame first entered human consciousness with the knowledge of good and evil which leads to death. Prior to this deadly knowledge, we lived in the innocent state of blissful exposure before God, "naked and not ashamed." With the choosing of knowledge, our nakedness was exposed and we became shame's puppet. Like a living burden, shame drives us to find a scapegoat. Its quantity, mass and weight are too heavy to be borne; it must be off-loaded.

Betrayal has allowed you to become your betrayer's scapegoat, their shame "shiftee." Your response has eternal implications for you and them. Will you bear your betrayer's shame? Will you offer the other cheek? Will you open not your mouth? Will you give your betrayer double what they ask?

No. You are not able.

Only Christ in you can love with *agape*. Will you let Him, through you, carry your betrayer's shame?

Yes. Yes, you will.

You assent. You want to fully know the love of Christ even if it requires the fellowship of His sufferings. You see the glory in experiencing all Christ's capacities for *agape*.

Your witness-bearing for Jesus is your chief concern, and you cannot be stopped in it till it is finished; therefore, be at peace. Cruel slander, wicked misrepresentation, desertion of friends, betrayal by the most trusted one, and whatever else may come, cannot hinder the Lord's purpose concerning you. The Lord stands by you in the night of your sorrow, and He says, "Thou must yet bear witness for me." Be calm; be filled with joy in the Lord.

If you do not need this promise just now, you may very soon. Treasure it up. Remember also to pray for missionaries and all persecuted ones, that the Lord would preserve them even to the completion of their lifework.

— Charles Spurgeon (1834-1892)

YOU: EXCHANGING FALSE ACCUSATION

It comes out of nowhere, like an arrow straight to your heart. Your innocence causes you to puzzle over the undeserved sting. For a time, you plan your defense and, attorney-like, you build an airtight case against the claims of your accuser. Then, in word and letter you make your defense only to find your accuser unhearing, unimpressed, unrelenting. You turn to others detailing your innocence but the comfort of their sympathy is fleeting and unhealing.

False accusation.

It can be as simple as a private misunderstanding or as major as a public slander. Both invade your life like an unwanted swarm of locusts eating up your good Christian name.

You suffer. Your accuser doesn't.

You assume that relief lies in your accuser's recanting and apologizing in full view of all who've heard and believed the false words. And yet, you know this will require a supernatural intervention to move your accuser's will, and prayers to that effect have gone unanswered. You cry, "God! Why don't you care about my reputation? My loss is Your loss. My loss is Your Kingdom's loss!"

He answers,

> *"Blessed are you when people insult you and persecute you, and falsely say all kinds of evil against you because of Me. Rejoice and be glad, for your reward in heaven is great; for in the same way they persecuted the prophets who were before you."*

— Matthew 5:11

In cultures where violence is frowned upon, words are the chosen weapons. God allows His Beloved to suffer others' words. He allows words to become the tearing scourge upon your back and the piercing thorns into your scalp. Take heart, Beloved; do not despair–treasure is there.

Your assent to false accusation is an assent to a piercing which allows your blood to flow. There, you are admitted into the fellowship of the pierced but innocent Christ. Also there, you are cleansed of your infection of self-interest which allows you a place of cleansing intercession on behalf of your accuser.

Still. You hesitate. The injustice is too hard to bear. You tell God, "Lies should never triumph. Truth should have the victory."

He answers, again,

> *"Blessed are you when men hate you, and ostracize you, and*
> *insult you, and scorn your name as evil, for the sake of the Son*
> *of Man. Be glad in that day and leap for joy, for behold, your*
> *reward is great in heaven. For in the same way their fathers used*
> *to treat the prophets."*
>
> — Luke 6:22-23

You don't feel glad or like leaping for joy. And you'd rather curse than bless your accuser.

Will you assent to the exchange of your right for justice for something eternal?

Yes, yes you will.

You're a child of the Kingdom of God and your obedience allows your King's will to be done on earth as it is in heaven. Often you won't understand the "why's" but Christ's words are clear to the falsely accused:

You are blessed.

You are to be glad.

You are to leap for joy.

You are to trust that your reward in heaven is great.

And when you do all that Christ commands, you come to accept that your accuser is a sacred tool in His hand, pruning deadness away to allow His love to flow through you, to pierce the intangible darkness of Satan's kingdom, and bear fruit eternal in the heavens.

For we know that if the earthly tent which is our house is torn down, we have a building from God, a house not made with hands, eternal in the heavens. For indeed in this house we groan, longing to be clothed with our dwelling from heaven, inasmuch as we, having put it on, will not be found naked. For indeed while we are in this tent, we groan, being burdened, because we do not want to be unclothed but to be clothed, so that what is mortal will be swallowed up by life. Now He who prepared us for this very purpose is God, who gave to us the Spirit as a pledge. Therefore, being always of good courage, and knowing that while we are at home in the body we are absent from the Lord–for we walk by faith, not by sight–we are of good courage, I say, and prefer rather to be absent from the body and to be at home with the Lord. Therefore we also have as our ambition, whether at home or absent, to be pleasing to Him. For we must all appear before the judgment seat of Christ, so that each one may be recompensed for his deeds in the body, according to what he has done, whether good or bad.

— 2 Corinthians 5:1-10

The furnace of affliction is a good place for you, Christian; it benefits you; it helps you to become more like Christ, and it is fitting you for heaven.

— Charles Spurgeon (1834-1892)

You: Exchanging Unanswered Prayer

You're confused. You've prayed the Bible's promises and you've asked others to do the same, both to no avail. Still, you pray with unrelenting vigor and courage, confident that God's lack of response is only a test of your persistence. You read Christian how-to books and get creative.

Weeks turn into months and the small, disputable answers to your prayers leave you filled with nagging doubts.

Maybe it was the medicines.

Maybe I didn't interview well.

Maybe we shouldn't have spent that money.

Maybe she will die.

Maybe I will die.

Doubts. At first, you have the strength to push them away like you would a pesky insect seeking to drain you of your life's blood. Doubts are powerful; they mean the end of your ability to control the hand of God—a terrifying prospect.

Or is it?

This is the beginning of an exchange.

Will you assent to listening to God rather than telling God? Even if it means loss in this realm?

Yes, yes you will.

In God's Kingdom, nothing can separate you from His love. Though you have equated some of this realm's perishables with His love and even prayed against their loss, you sense a calling to ascend above their earthly pull. There, you find your needs are met by eating and drinking of Christ.

True prayer, as in justifying faith, is an assenting to that which is already done. How can one know if the thing has been done? By the word spoken to you by the Holy Spirit. Once that word is spoken, the thing is done, created, finished.

> You have to know what God is thinking about a matter; that is, to ascertain the mind of God. And if you walk in the Spirit and commune with Him, He can communicate with you and all you need to do is to abide in that one little word which He speaks to your heart, letting all the other promises go. All you need to do is to place your faith in that one little word which He has given concerning the thing that is before you. Do that which He says to you and not forty other things. Believe that what He is saying is what He wants you to believe. Go before Him and say,
>
> "Father, here is a situation. I could get twenty-five promises out of the Bible, but I refuse to do that because I have been defeated too many times by following that method. Lord, what do You desire in this matter? Intimate Your will to my

poor troubled heart; just one word. Whisper to me in my spirit the attitude that You wish me to take and if it be Your good pleasure bring to my mind a promise, an intimation which will grip me as a conviction. Perhaps you can bring me into contact with someone who will be a voice for me. God, speak to me. You are intelligent; I am but a child, but You say that Your sheep know Your voice. What is Your thought about this situation? All I want is to take the right attitude towards it."

— John Wright Follette (1883-1966), *The Rule of Three*

YOU: EXCHANGING MINISTRY DISILLUSIONMENT

Your days are filled with burdensome chores and thoughts. You slog on, day after day, month after month, year after year. If you could, you'd like to quit ministry but how can you face a future without purpose?

Disillusionment.

You began with high hopes, literally. The prospect of doing something important for God lifted you from the doldrums of nagging doubts, nagging depression and nagging shame. Feeling useful, spiritual, and exceptional, you forged ahead without a care and nary a prayer.

Good results ensued: people were taught, fed, clothed and cheered and complimentary public feedback reached your ears. All was well . . . until it wasn't. The one-time needs you thought you'd met became perpetual, money became scarce and helpers became transient or undependable. Discouraged, you turned your anger on your inactive brethren's inattention, covetousness and disobedience.

Will you exchange doing good works for sitting before Christ?

Are you willing to wait to hear?

Are you willing to obey what you hear?

Yes. Yes, you are.

You are a child of the Kingdom. Your nature pulls you in a new, living, eternal direction. The discerning of spirit from flesh is upon you like never before. Clearly the burden of mitigating the unending needs of the unredeemed wasn't your Kingdom mission.

You repent. You reckon your best attempts to serve Him are without wisdom and only serve to muddy the face of Christ. You feel deep sorrow. You let go with childlike trust. You wait on God and no longer assume.

He promises, "All things together for your good," and further, "that nothing can separate you from His love."

In this humble state of seeking God before doing for God, you are rightly aligned as the branch described in John 15. As you remain in submission to the processes of the Kingdom of God within, you bring forth real fruit. As you submit to pruning, dead works fall away and living works are expressed through you:

Love

Joy

Peace

Gentleness

Goodness

Faithfulness

Kindness

Patience

Self-control

The redeemed nature! What all creation has been in expectant labor to bring forth—the Sons of God! Like a city set on a hill, you are the light of the world offering the only hope for man: redemption from sin through Christ.

> Since all that I meet
> Shall work for my good,
> The bitter is sweet,
> The med'cine is food;
> Though painful at present,
> Wilt cease before long,
> And then, O! how pleasant,
> The conqueror's song!
>
> — John Newton (1725-1807), *Olney Hymns*

YOU: EXCHANGING BURNOUT

You're tired, even hateful, of your job. People ask you too often if you're tired. Your heart races when the phone rings. You're happy when a cold or flu sends you to bed. Ministry has become drudgery.

Burnout.

Half of ministers wish they could do something else. The relentless demands, impossible expectations and discouraging in-effectiveness are beyond human strength. You may have thought you'd be different but you're not. You're over your head, literally.

The health of the Body of Christ is a delicate balance of each part serving and complementing the other parts. The Holy Spirit gifted you specifically, uniquely, for the health of the whole. When you took on more than Christ required, you not only found the grace to be fruitful absent, the more needs you took on, the less the Body functioned. This left you angry and frustrated. You dele-gated and restructured but still found you often resorted to shame to motivate others. This worked sometimes but never to the level that you desired. Time went by and ministry lost its charm; Christ's promise of a burden "easy and light" escaped your experience.

Two answering paths became clear:

Keep on keeping-on

Quit

If the perceived shame of quitting was too costly, or the losing of your livelihood too scary, you kept-on, barely sustained by the occasional fruit you produced. You concluded that the joylessness you experienced was the result of the spread-too-thin-doers doing the work intended for all.

If you were weakened beyond your ability to resist, your dreams of importance for God died. Humbled, you sat at Christ's feet ready to receive "that good part." The Holy Spirit fed you truths you'd missed. He brought back to your painful remembrance the dozens of occasions you'd failed to gain the Father's permission before you acted. He exposed your coveting of more and the doing of more because you'd independently decided it felt right and good. He whispered, "My child, you are careful and troubled about many things unintended. In giving out more than I give you, your own health and the health of My Body suffers."

Christ offered an exchange: for the giving up of your home-made bread, Christ gave you Living Bread which you would, in time, break to feed others. For the giving up of homemade wine, Christ filled you with new wine which would, in time, become streams of Living Water flowing from your belly.

You assented to the proper order and discovered new-found joy in the yoke of life and ministry. It is in the fires of suffering that God purifies His saints and brings them to the highest things. It is in the furnace their faith is tested, their patience is tried, and they are developed in all those rich virtues which make up Christian character. It is while they are passing through deep waters that He shows how close He can come to His praying, believing saints.

— E. M. Bounds (1835-1913), *Essentials of Prayer*

YOU: EXCHANGING YOU

You've changed; your misaligned self-interest has suffered a fatal blow and the interests of the Father reign. Christianity no longer serves as a way for you to get God to align Himself with your interests. No, quite the opposite.

It's official–the Kingdom's nursery walls are behind you. You are a city set on a hill–ZION.

Now, when you address the Father, you long to avoid the confusing grief of unanswered, misaligned prayers. You listen more and assume less. You search the scriptures and conclude that you know very little about the mysteries of the Kingdom of God. The Lord's instruction to pray, "Thy Kingdom come, Thy will be done on earth," becomes significant for its implications.

> *And turning His gaze toward His disciples, He began to say, "Blessed are you who are poor, for yours is the kingdom of God. Blessed are you who hunger now, for you shall be satisfied. Blessed are you who weep now, for you shall laugh. Blessed are you when men hate you, and ostracize you, and insult you, and scorn your name as evil, for the sake of the Son of Man. Be glad in that day and leap for joy, for behold, your reward is great in heaven. For in the same way their fathers used to treat the prophets."*
>
> — Luke 6:20-23

> *And Jesus, looking around, said to His disciples, "How hard it will be for those who are wealthy to enter the kingdom of God!" The disciples were amazed at His words. But Jesus answered again and said to them, "Children, how hard it is to enter the kingdom of God! It is easier for a camel to go through the eye of a needle than for a rich man to enter the kingdom of God."*

They were even more astonished and said to Him, "Then who can
be saved?" Looking at them, Jesus said, "With people it is impos-
sible, but not with God; for all things are possible with God."

— Mark 10:23-27

Need.

Inadequacy.

Narrow roads few want to travel.

But you now see that instances of physical need have become
paths to the hidden treasures of God. You see all instances of emotional need have become paths to knowing the love of Christ. Your
first resistance to Kingdom Exchanges has given way to a new,
though tentative, sometimes wary, hopefulness.

> *Therefore, having been justified by faith, we have peace*
> *with God through our Lord Jesus Christ, through whom also*
> *we have obtained our introduction by faith into this grace in*
> *which we stand; and we exult in hope of the glory of God. And*
> *not only this, but we also exult in our tribulations, knowing that*
> *tribulation brings about perseverance; and perseverance, proven*
> *character; and proven character, hope; and hope does not disap-*
> *point, because the love of God has been poured out within our*
> *hearts through the Holy Spirit who was given to us.*
>
> — Romans 5:1-5

Will you exchange yourself?

Yes, yes you will.

Though you're scared, uncertain and a bit cranky, when you
assent to God's offerings, you understand His love far exceeds your
understanding. God gives by taking away and those eternal truths

you gained are now held in your thankful heart. You know God more. You love God more. You trust God more. You understand the hope described in Romans 5–the kind of hope that comes from you ending your tribulation season with more of Christ than when you began.

Your heart sings, "Oh, the love of God! A love that pours such glories into the void that sacrifice fears unfillable."

> I cannot choose so as to decline the thing; I must through much tribulation enter into the kingdom of God. (Acts 14:22) Therefore I will labour, not to be like a young colt, first set to plough, which more tires himself out with his own untoward-ness (whipping himself with his misspent mettle) than with the weight of what he draws: and will labour patiently to bear what is imposed upon me.

> — Thomas Fuller (1608-1661), *Good Thoughts in Bad Times*

PART IV

HOUSEKEEPING THE STRUCTURE WITH CHRIST

YOU: MISSING AN EXCHANGE

You thought you got the victory. You did. You got what you wanted, you needed, couldn't live without. It took imagination, effort and lots of time but by this realm's standards you did it!

But, inside, you feel empty and uneasy. Why the void? Why does your brow still furrow?

Because you missed it. In fact, you did the very things Christ warned against. Instead of an exchange for Christ's glory, you chose your reputation, your comfort, your security, your happiness. This is why you slump with the malaise of lost gain.

Offerings of glory are offered not pushed. Though you missed an opportunity to honor the memory of Christ by becoming broken bread and poured out wine, you didn't lose your salvation. You lost an opportunity to love as Christ and thereby to share that portion of inheritance He offered.

Your suffering spirit is raw for truth to reign and your words of confession are its healing balm. Confession divides like a surgeon's scalpel; you will feel it separating the true life you have in Christ from the carnal life you're scared to lose.

Mourn over your loss of glory as over a pearl of great price, a lost coin, a treasure hidden in that field you didn't buy and you will be set free to face future exchanges with Truth reigning in your mortal body.

You will have future opportunities for exchanges. Of that there is no doubt. Imagine them. Plan for them. Prepare for them. Practice your response now, before the stress and confusion descends and scrambles your resolve to overcome. Overcoming is natural for your spirit and preparing for your spirit to have the last word is vital. In the end, after many exchanges you will, with Paul, proclaim,

> *I count all things to be loss in view of the surpassing value*
> *of knowing Christ Jesus my Lord, for whom I have suffered the*
> *loss of all things, and count them but rubbish so that I may gain*
> *Christ.*
>
> — Philippians 3:8

Surely it is reasonable to fling away paste pearls for real ones. Surely it is reasonable to fling away brass counters for gold coins. Surely, in all regions of life, we willingly sacrifice the second best in order to get the very best. Surely if the wealth which is in God is more precious than all besides, you have the best of the bargain, if you part with the world and yourselves and get Him.

— Alexander MacLaren (1826-1910)
Expositions of Holy Scripture

YOU: GETTING THE MOST OUT OF EXCHANGES

You are there. You have exchanged what the world gives for what your Father in Heaven gives.

What you supposed was great loss has turned into a cold drink of which you partake. What began as a slow trickle of truth has become a well from which you draw Living Water. Your relief is tangible and measureable. The temptation to grieve your losses as one without hope in an unseen Kingdom lessens until it is a fleeting temptation quickly resisted by the shield of faith that you raise to block Satan's fiery darts.

You have a testimony. Write it down. Share it as you would an abundance of food–with discretion–and the truth you've been given will spring from you, giving life to others.

It's not an option to bury away the Kingdom talent you've been given. Christ planted is Christ reaped. As an in-love servant of the King, your planting of The Way, The Truth and The Life is your only truly productive, grow-able talent.

YOU: COMFORTING OTHERS DURING THEIR EXCHANGES

You've been at that place of tribulation and watching a brother or sister suffer is disturbing. You remember the process–the slow dying to self. You remember the crying, the pleading, the hope lost. But you also remember the fruit born, the glory you received. You wonder what you can do to ease or possibly shorten the process for your fellow pilgrim.

Blessed be the God and Father of our Lord Jesus Christ, the Father of mercies and God of all comfort, who comforts us in all our affliction so that we will be able to comfort those who are in any affliction with the comfort with which we ourselves are comforted by God.

— 2 Corinthians 1:3-4

Come alongside. The day will come when the ground of the suffering heart will be prepared to receive. Your words will come forth naturally and be watered by your love, but unlike the unseeing words of those who wish to comfort by claiming removal of the sufferer's trial, your words will not confuse the sufferer with false hope. Your words will find fertile ground, plowed and ready for an assent to the eternal in order to become a glorious overcomer.

Your experience as a comforter will mature with anointing and experience. The days of great trial that arise during the final tests, which are purposed to reveal the goats and sheep and the wheat and the tares will be as to you a grand and rich harvest where all that you have acquired through your assents will be a warm balm easing the sore and weary.

Behold, the LORD lays the earth waste, devastates it, distorts its surface and scatters its inhabitants. And the people will be like the priest, the servant like his master, the maid like her mistress, the buyer like the seller, the lender like the borrower, the creditor like the debtor. The earth will be completely laid waste and completely despoiled, for the LORD has spoken this word. The earth mourns and withers, the world fades and withers, the exalted of the people of the earth fade away. The earth is also polluted by its inhabitants, for they transgressed laws, violated statutes, broke the everlasting covenant. Therefore, a curse devours the earth, and those who live in it are held guilty. Therefore, the inhabitants of the earth are burned, and few men are left.

The new wine mourns, The vine decays,
All the merry-hearted sigh.
The gaiety of tambourines ceases,
The noise of revelers stops,
The gaiety of the harp ceases.
They do not drink wine with song;
Strong drink is bitter to those who drink it.
The city of chaos is broken down;
Every house is shut up so that none may enter.
There is an outcry in the streets concerning the wine;
All joy turns to gloom. The gaiety of the earth is banished.
Desolation is left in the city
And the gate is battered to ruins.
For thus it will be in the midst of the earth among the peoples,
As the shaking of an olive tree,
As the gleanings when the grape harvest is over.
They raise their voices, they shout for joy;
They cry out from the west concerning the majesty of the LORD.
Therefore glorify the LORD in the east,
The name of the LORD, the God of Israel,
In the coastlands of the sea.
From the ends of the earth we hear songs, "Glory to the Righteous One."

— Isaiah 24:1-16

Goats separated, tares burned, you—the sheep and the wheat—sing praises to the Righteous One, Who was willing to set aside His glory in order that you might share His glory.

Part V
The Structure Full of God's Glory

YOU: Complete and Presentable without Spot or Wrinkle

Everything you assent to lose
Christ fills with Himself
Bread and wine you become
Sacrificed for others
His will done on earth as it is in heaven.

The Word, the Lamb Who was slain before the foundations of the earth, spoke into existence this laboring creation. With patient groaning, the creation travails for the sons of men to reveal God's image. These sons have one allegiance, one devotion, one purpose: God's Kingdom. They are in the world but not of the world. They have sacrificed their natural affections, strength, and way of thinking to find God's heart, God's strength, and God's mind.

The exchange rate? 1 equals 100.

Your Kingdom inheritance begins now—in this realm. It's not a transient, material inheritance and though you may know seasons of material blessing and plenty, you will find greater blessings in seasons of want. Want is the catalyst which exposes the perishable and reveals the eternal.

*Peter began to say to Him, "Behold, we have left everything
and followed You." Jesus said, "Truly I say to you, there is no one
who has left house or brothers or sisters or mother or father or
children or farms, for My sake and for the gospel's sake, but that
he will receive a hundred times as much now in the present age,
houses and brothers and sisters and mothers and children and
farms, along with persecutions; and in the age to come, eternal
life. But many who are first will be last, and the last, first."*

— Mark 10:28-31

You are the keeper of God's interests.

You need tools.

And God imparts these tools to pull down this realm's spiritual
strongholds, imaginations, and everything that exalts itself above
the knowledge of God. Through you, the light of truth exposes the
underbelly of Satan's lies and when your obediences are fulfilled,
you are able to take captive even disobedient thoughts in order to
deliver them to the obedience of Christ. Then, you shall shine forth
as the sun in the Kingdom of your Father.

THE SUM OF ALL EXCHANGES: BECOMING BREAD AND WINE

Grain and Grapes. Good, in and of themselves, but once transformed into bread and wine, very much preferred.

A kernel of grain crushed and lost to become bread.

A single grape crushed and lost to become wine.

*And He said to them, "I have earnestly desired to eat this
Passover with you before I suffer; for I say to you, I shall never*

again eat it until it is fulfilled in the kingdom of God." And
when He had taken a cup and given thanks, He said, "Take this
and share it among yourselves; for I say to you, I will not drink
of the fruit of the vine from now on until the kingdom of God
comes." And when He had taken some bread and given thanks,
He broke it and gave it to them, saying, "This is My body which
is given for you; do this in remembrance of Me." And in the
same way He took the cup after they had eaten, saying, "This cup
which is poured out for you is the new covenant in My blood."

— Luke 22:15-20

You began your Kingdom life as an individual grain, an individual grape, added to others. Through trials and tribulations you have been crushed of self-interest to become bread and wine poured out for others in remembrance of Christ.

The "I's" disappear from your thoughts, words and writings.

Carnal perishables tempt but aren't given satisfaction.

Kingdom treasure is your preference.

Loss exchanged for overcoming.

Aloneness exchanged for fellowship with Christ.

Failure exchanged for gold, silver and precious stones.

Rejection exchanged for agape.

Confusion and uncertainty exchanged for trust.

Sickness, disease and disability exchanged for humility, freedom from bondage, fellowship with Christ and the health of the Body of Christ.

Captivity exchanged for the freedom of others.

Poverty exchanged for eternal treasure.

Persecution exchanged for a share in Christ's love.

Impatience exchanged for waiting on God.

Spiritual covetousness exchanged for the health of the Body of Christ.

Betrayal exchanged for fellowship in Christ's sufferings.

False accusation exchanged for blessings, gladness, joy, and heavenly reward.

Unanswered prayer exchanged for God's desires.

Disillusionment exchanged for lasting fruit.

Burnout exchanged for streams of living water flowing from you.

You, exchanged for the glory of Christ in you.

> *Grace to you and peace, from Him who is and who was and who is to come, and from the seven Spirits who are before His throne, and from Jesus Christ, the faithful witness, the first-born of the dead, and the ruler of the kings of the earth. To Him who loves us and released us from our sins by His blood and has made us to be a kingdom, priests to His God and Father—to Him be the glory and the dominion forever and ever. Amen.*

> — Revelation 1:4-6

This hill though high I covet to ascend;

The difficulty will not me offend;

For I perceive the way of life here.

Come, pluck up, heart; let's neither faint nor fear.

> — John Bunyan (1628-1688) *The Pilgrim's Progress*

MOSAIC

jagged shards of self-esteem
battered brittle bits of dreams
splinters of declining wealth
shattered glass of broken health
fragile, faltering, fractured prayer
hardened hopes dashed in despair
vanishing, vanquished expectation
reaching up in desperation
who can salvage scraps like these?
to bring some comfort and appease.
who can gather the debris
and make it beautiful for me?
I am the Artist of your soul.

I'll re-design and make it whole.
Relinquish to Me every care.
Release the things that laid you bare.
These broken pieces I can use
To form true beauty, if you choose.
I'll gather all that has been shattered,
And create a lovely pattern.
My love will make from stones of strife,
A graced mosaic of your life.

— *Susan Estribou Ramsden*

More from Energion Publications

Personal Study

Holy Smoke! Unholy Fire	Bob McKibben	$14.99
The Jesus Paradigm	David Alan Black	$17.99
When People Speak for God	Henry Neufeld	$17.99
The Sacred Journey	Chris Surber	$11.99

Christian Living

It's All Greek to Me	David Alan Black	$3.99
Grief: Finding the Candle of Light	Jody Neufeld	$8.99
Hunger: Satisfying the Longing of Your Soul	Jon L. Dybdahl	$12.99
My Life Story	Becky Lynn Black	$14.99
Crossing the Street	Robert LaRochelle	$16.99
The Spirit's Fruit	David Moffett-Moore	$9.99
Holistic Spirituality	Bruce G. Epperly	$4.99

Bible Study

Learning and Living Scripture	Lentz/Neufeld	$12.99
Galatians: A Participatory Study Guide	Bruce Epperly	$9.99
Ephesians: A Participatory Study Guide	Robert D. Cornwall	$9.99
Ecclesiastes: A Participatory Study Guide	Russell Meek	$9.99

Theology

Creation in Scripture	Herold Weiss	$12.99
Creation: the Christian Doctrine	Edward W. H. Vick	$12.99
The Character of Our Discontent	Allan R. Bevere	$12.99
Ultimate Allegiance	Robert D. Cornwall	$9.99
The Journey to the Undiscovered Country	William Powell Tuck	$9.99
Process Theology	Bruce G. Epperly	$4.99

Ministry

Clergy Table Talk	Kent Ira Groff	$9.99
Thrive: Spritual Habits of Transforming Congregations	Ruth A. Fletcher	$14.99

Generous Quantity Discounts Available
Dealer Inquiries Welcome
Energion Publications — P.O. Box 841
Gonzalez, FL 32560
Website: http://energionpubs.com
Phone: (850) 525-3916

www.ingramcontent.com/pod-product-compliance
Lightning Source LLC
Chambersburg PA
CBHW031625040426
42452CB00007B/683